Hector A. Stuart

Ben Nebo

A Pilgrimage in the South Seas

Hector A. Stuart

Ben Nebo
A Pilgrimage in the South Seas

ISBN/EAN: 9783744652827

Printed in Europe, USA, Canada, Australia, Japan

Cover: Foto ©ninafisch / pixelio.de

More available books at **www.hansebooks.com**

BEN NEBO;

A PILGRIMAGE IN THE SOUTH SEAS.

IN THREE CANTOS.

By H. A. STUART.

[CALIBAN.]

SAN FRANCISCO:

PRINTED AND PUBLISHED BY WADE AND COMPANY, 411 CLAY ST.

1871.

NOTES.

"THE THREE KINGS THESE! INFIXED AMID THE FLOOD."
Page 7; verse 1.

A few leagues beyond the coast of the northern island of New Zealand, are three stupendous rocks, rising like turrets, from the sea. They are visible at a vast distance; and, seen under a tempestuous sunset, present a spectacle of singular magnificence.

"'TWAS DARING TASMAN AND HIS ROVING CREW WHO FIRST THESE ISLANDS IN THEIR WANDERINGS FOUND."
Page 12; verse 3.

New Zealand was first discovered by Tasman in 1642, but he did not land. The natives, however, came on board, and some intercourse took place, during which seven of the Dutch who had gone ashore were cruelly slaughtered. The great navigator Cook explored these regions in 1770, and discovered a strait which divides the country into two large islands. The southern was called by the natives Tavia Poenamoo, and the northern Eaheianowmawe, names which equal the Russian in length, and which might well be contracted. The first is not less than 600 B. miles in length, by 150 in medial breadth; and the second is little inferior in size.

"THESE ISLES ARE BY BOON NATURE WITH RICH GIFTS ENDOWED."
Page 12; verse 4.

The islands of New Zealand enjoy a temperate climate, similar to that of France. The soil is exceedingly fertile, and is found to contain minerals, of which gold is the most abundant. The natives were—and in some parts are still—cannibals. They are of a brown complexion, little deeper than the Spanish, and many are even fair. They equal the tallest Europeans in stature; and their features are commonly regular and pleasing. It is singular to observe such a diversity between them and the natives of Australia, when theory would expect to find them the same race of men. So far as present discoveries extend, the natives of Australia and Papua seem to display an African origin; while most of the other islands in the Pacific appear to have been peopled from Asia.

"THIS MAORI DREAD WHERE MANY CHIEFS HAD DIED."
Page 13; verse 2.

A misprint: it should be Morai. The Morais are places of worship where the aged are frequently left to perish. They are usually lawns shaded by trees esteemed sacred. Among these the crateva or purataruru, the terminalia glabra or tara iri, and the dracena terminalis, are the principal. Caves are occasionally used.

"IN GLEAMING JAD AND MARO WHITE ARRAY'D."
Page 13; verse 3.

Jad—a green stone wrought by the natives into ornaments and rude tools, with the latter of which they are ingenious mechanics. Maro—a narrow piece of coarse cloth formed of flax, in the same manner as at Otaheite. It is passed between the legs and fastened round the loins. In battle the men throw a kind of mats over their shoulders; and this armor is neatly manufactured. On solemn occasions the chiefs wear dresses ingeniously composed of feathers. The women have only a slight wrapper; and the hair is cut short behind but turned up from their forehead. The ears are ornamented with bits of jad or beads, the face being often besmeared with a red paint, seemingly iron ochre mingled with grease. The heroic actions of their sires are perpetuated in legend; the voice being accompanied by a rude instrument, shapen like a lyre.

"AND FIXED FOR SEA THEIR LENGTHY BARGES LAY."
Page 15; verse 2.

The canoes of the New Zealanders are well built of planks, raised upon each other, and fastened with strong withes. Some are fifty feet long, and so broad as to be able to sail without an out-rigger, but the smaller sort commonly have one, and they often fasten two together by rafters. The large canoes will carry thirty men or more; and have often a head ingeniously carved.

"THUS, WHEN IN DEATH A MAORI LIETH STARK."
Page 19; verse 1.

The New Zealanders inter their dead; they also believe that three days after the interment the heart separates itself from the corpse, and, concealed in a shell of bark, is carried to the clouds by an attendant spirit. A queer belief, truly, yet not more preposterous than some of our more civilized imaginings.

"AND SUICIDE, THAT RATHER DOUBTFUL ACT."
Page 19; verse 3.

Suicide is very common among the Maoris, and this they often commit by hanging themselves on the slightest occasions. A woman who has been punished by her husband, will very likely put an end to further chastisements by the aid of a halter.

V

"HE ATE A WHOLE BOAT'S CREW AND MADE A DEATHLESS FAME."
Page 21; verse 3.

The New Zealanders, as before remarked, are cannibals, unless where christianity has exerted its civilizing influence. The bodies of their enemies, while yet warm, are cut in pieces, broiled and devoured with peculiar satisfaction. I knew a chief in Auckland, who vowed that he had assisted in devouring a party of Cook's men, who were surprised near Adventure Bay. He dwelt on that feast with profound interest; for it seems "tarpaulins" are not bad eating; and a cabin-boy is said to taste like young opossum.

"PRIME OVER ALL THE ARTOCARPUS REIGNS—
MAJESTIC MONARCH OF THE TORRID ZONE."
Page 30; verse 3.

Of the plants peculiar to the tropical islands, the chief is the Artocarpus, or bread fruit. This valuable tree rises to the hight of more than forty feet, with a trunk the thickness of a man's body. Its fruit, which is about the size of a twenty-four pound shot, when roasted is a most wholesome nourishment, and in taste resembles new wheaten bread. For eight successive months every year does this tree continue to furnish fruit in such abundance that three of them are sufficient for the support of one man: nor is this the whole of its value; the inner bark is manufactured into cloth, the wood is excellent for the construction of huts and canoes, the leaves serve instead of dishes, and of its milky glutinous juice a tenacious cement and bird-lime is prepared.

ERRATUM. Page 32; verse 2. For ' enchance'' read "enhance."

INTRODUCTION.

PEOPLE in these times are not supposed to rank poetry too highly; yet there are some who are not above verse, and to these BEN NEBO is directed. Of the Poem itself I shall say nothing: its conduct lies among the South Seas; and so far as the description of the natives, islands, adventures, etc. are concerned, is strictly correct—all being drawn from personal experience.

Ben Nebo is an imaginary name compounded for the occasion. Nebo, as the intelligent reader is aware, is the name of one of the summits of the mountains of Abarim, whence the great Hebrew legislator was permitted to behold the Land of Promise, before yielding up his spirit. I chose the name because it struck me as unique and euphonius: the prefix "Ben" is simply an abbreviation of Benjamin—a style I have also adopted from mere novelty, and which is seen in other names in the poem, thus: Ned Bastion, Dave Vangs, etc. I trust no harm will come of this innovation, though perhaps more toploftical titles might have a better effect in a rhyming production; but if the characters are proper, who will quarrel with patronymics?

Ben Nebo, himself, is a fanciful character, created for the purpose of effect, and is supposed to be the super-cargo of the trader. He may be a rather cynical and unamiable personage; but for this I am not accountable; no author is responsible for the vagaries of his creations.

This volume contains but a fragment of his adventures; should it meet with favorable consideration I may follow it with another. Its reception will decide whether I may venture to remove the hero from the Pirate Isle, and, conducting him through a series of events, restore him to his native land: these three cantos are merely experimental.

As regards the manner of the verse, I have chosen that of Spenser; because, of all other styles that I know of, it admits of the greatest variation; and is, therefore, eminently adapted to a subject like this, which is somewhat changeable and excursive. Should failure ensue, it must lie rather in the execution than in the design, which has been sanctioned by many of our greatest poets, among them Ariosto, Thomson, Beattie, and the mightier endorsement of Byron.

The illustrations are photographed by Messrs. Flaglor and Perkins from original designs made by the leading artists of San Francisco: Fortunato Arriola, G. J. Denny, R. G. Holdredge, Ed. Richardson, L. F. Ireland, Frederick Whymper, John M. Tracy, Charles Rodgers, Eugene A. Poole and Pascal Loomis, are represented by characteristic drawings.

I have now done with Ben Nebo; and, while I feel a pang at parting with so familiar an associate, I trust he may be able to outlive the storms which frequently beset a new navigator in the seas of literature. Allah il Allah.

S.

DEDICATION.

Thomas B. Lewis, Esq.,

DEAR SIR:

The following Poem being finished and about to make an entrance into the world, I know of no name among my circle of acquaintance so fitted to honor its inscription-page as your own. Although selfish reasons might bias many in selecting a name so extensively and favorably known, yet I have other and nobler considerations in placing it at the head of this volume. Aside from the promptings of friendship, your qualities as a man and a citizen would suffice to claim a tribute like this; but over all there rests a weightier consideration—your generous but unobtrusive patronage of art and literature. I question whether there is a man in the State, who "in a silent way" has done more to promote these two branches: I might give instances but they are not necessary.

As a token of the esteem in which I hold those qualities, I offer to your acceptance the following Poem; and with the wish that it may receive your approbation,

I subscribe myself,

Your obliged and sincere friend,

H. A. STUART.

San Francisco, Oct. 23, 1870.

BEN NEBO;

A PILGRIMAGE IN THE SOUTH SEAS.

CANTO I.

RETIRED within this gloomy cave, that stands
    All lonely on the sad, sea-beaten shore,
'Tis mine to sing of Ascian's glowing lands—
    To plow again her sparkling waters o'er,
    And from Oblivion strange events restore.
And as the Genius of th' eventful song
    Exultant springs his mingled tones to pour,
Deep-hidden deeds in every whisper throng,
And chanting Pity weeps as roll the strains along.

The sun is red on Australs' flashing main,
    And fresh the wind that curls the rushing foam;
No more inert! Upheave the lengthened chain!
    We must away o'er distant seas to roam;
    Self-exiled from our fair and much-loved home.
On deck Ben Nebo stood, and sadder grew
    As darker evening's curtain 'gan to loam;
And oft he sighed, as o'er the surges blue
The fond familiar land receded from his view.

Now out upon the open sea we ride,
    And to the pressing gale the vessel bends;
Her sturdy bows push headlong through the tide,
    And far beyond her tapering shade extends,
    As deep astern the lurid sun descends;
While round the mast the sea-gull circling flies,
    And to the watch his dirgeful murmur sends,
Till his untiring wing sidelong he plies,
And melts in gloom as Eve forsakes the dark'ning skies.

Beyond the boiling wake, his eyes in vain
    Ben Nebo cast to view the fading shore,
But shadows loom along the leaden main,
    And doubtful outlines gloam the distance o'er,
    Where waves on waves in chilling fury roar.
His native land has melted from his sight,
    But Recollection can its scenes restore;
Yet many a joyous image cheers the night,
And weeping sorrows rise like phantoms to affright.

"Adieu, fair land! long years may first revolve
    Ere I again thy vernal meads shall tread—
The dreams of youth in frosty age dissolve,
    And new born pleasures mingle with the dead,
    As Time with chilly wind beats round my head;
Adieu, fair land! I love thee; yet 'twas thou
    Gave me this being which I so much dread;
'Twas thou sustained my infant steps, yet now
Self-exiled from thy shores, the wintry waves I plow.

"Yet why should I complain, since all are doomed
    To various toil by ruthless Destiny!
Some in the stifling cell, or mine, are tombed—
    Some rove neglected on the warring sea;
    Yet every fate is such as it should be.
Man is but dust in Fate's almighty eye,
    Though he may claim to immortality,
And deem he lives when dumb his ashes lie—
And none have e'er came back to tell him how to die.

"Man is but dust upon the wheel of life—
 As it revolves so he must circle round ;
He who resists—in the unequal strife—
 Is first into insensate powder ground,
 While still unstopp'd the tireless rim will bound.
Man's puny arm can naught of use avail,
 To clamp the law that Fate approveth sound,
At best he can his helpless state bewail,
Or, if foolhardy, at its mighty author rail."

Thus mused Ben Nebo, as across the skies
 He saw the stars their pathless courses thread—
The wondrous planets from the east arise,
 Or in the west their paling lustre shed ;
 While like a fiery serpent, overhead
A mighty comet meets his wondering sight,
 And fills the crew with superstitious dread;
Who in its vast array of ruddy light,
Behold some demon fell in flaming wrath bedight.

Majestic wanderer, wheeling through the gloom
 With none to guide thee in thy wayward flight,
What, as wind-fanned thy flames terrific loom,
 Doth lead thee through the dark involving night,
 Or steer thy bulk 'mongst countless spheres aright?
In orb erratic doomed for aye to sweep,
 And darkened nations with thy glance affright;
What fate is thine thus tireless on to leap,
And blast with quenchless fires the vast etherial deep?

In vain to ask : our thoughts to earth are prest,
 Though some inspiring wish exalts the soul
To rise above the grosser sense, and quest
 The mystic marvels that above us roll,
 Or deeper seek the spirit's subtle goal;
But ah! such flights a sober mind denies,
 Pleased with its little earthly-natured dole—
'Tis but the wandering thought that heavenward flies,
Or to pierce what is hid with pride presuming tries.

'Tis folly when the rigid will of Fate
    Has closed the Future to our darkened gaze,
To press obtrusive at the folded gate,
    And thread unasked the unfrequented maze;
    For, could we view its scenes, anguish might craze
Our souls; or we might see in dark distress
    No sign of bliss to cheer our ghostly days;
If like the ox, man is no more nor less—
Death snuffs the spark of life and all is nothingness.

But yet this cannot be; there is within
    This ashy casket something that will glow
When Earth has claimed her poor terrestrious kin,
    And all that lived is laid forever low!
    As dust no more of lingering grief to know,
A spark ignited at a deathless fire,
    A soul immortal, yet alive to woe
And bliss, still having that which will inspire
It with transcendent light when all its dregs expire.

'Tis this that lifts the man above the brute,
    Exalts his mind, and fires his soul with dreams
Bright and incarnate—the appointed fruit
    Of that celestial joy which ever teems
    In a well ordered mind—a mind that deems
Its great Creator the sole object worth
    A life-long adoration; such as streams
Spontaneous from the ruder tribes of earth
When in united strain they hail fair Nature's birth.

Sunk are the bulwarks of the winding lands—
    On every side the boundless sea extends;
Still like a statue fixed, Ben Nebo stands,
    And to the reckless gales his anguish sends—
    That anguish which his manly bosom rends;
For he was one whom Fate relentless casts
    Upon a troubled surge; nor joy descends
To shield him from the ever howling blasts
That shook his heart like winds a wreck's unsteady masts.

"Roll on ye waves! ye loud-voiced breezes blow!
  Your mournful sounds congenial strike my ear;
Although there falls betimes a note of woe—
  A mystic sound as spirit-voices drear
  That wail of pleasures lost and sorrows near;
Still, still! your gloomy diapasons roll,
  And bear me onward as ye swift career;
While in consonance with your cries, my soul
Shall mingling rise and sweep through Sorrow's pensive goal!

"Shades of the Past! why should your grisled forms
  Eternal haunt my vain-averted sight?
More woful ye than ocean's windy storms,
  Or shaft that thunders in the dreadful fight,
  Or bolt that hurtles in the dead of night;
These though, too oft with wrath unseemly fraught
  Smite at a blow, nor long the fated fright,
But ye with deathless pangs my soul hath taught
That of all barbs none vie with sorrow-haunting Thought.

"Here as I muse amid the whirlwind's wail,
  The sea's deep sob, the mew's complaining cry,
My heart pours out her melancholy tale
  Of buried joys that still uncovered lie,
  Though darkly sealed from each obtrusive eye.
And what is life to him whose bosom owns
  Such pangs as these that were not made to die?
In vain for respite he continual groans,
Or flies as from himself to earth's remotest zones."

But lo! the night is waning, and afar
  Morn's early blush comes dappling o'er the verge;
Now paler-gleams each white, translucent star,
  And fairer foams the onward-dashing surge;
  While from their watery beds, the gulls emerge,
And shivering sweep across the wide expanse.
  Still on her course fair winds the vessel urge,
As hope beams forth in every wanderer's glance,
And high each bosom beats as round the waters dance.

Fair was the voyage till on the hazy lee
  The Maori shores loomed like a belt of blue,
When darkly o'er the dim, north-western sea,
  A murky cloud rose ominous to view,
  And whistling winds in rising gamuts blew;
Anon across the wild, upsurging tides
  Storm-boding petrels in confusion flew;
And the fleet porpoise o'er the surges rides,
And far to calmer seas his shape unwieldy guides.

Firm at his post the sun-browned master stands,
  Yet views with awe yon wind-announcing cloud;
For on his lee appeared New Zealand's strands,
  Half-hid in one long, dark incumbent shroud,
  And far beyond with devious shoals endowed.
But still deep versant in the windy jar,
  He stood alert, though hoarse the tempest soughed,
And huge o'er many a circumjacent bar
The frothy breakers raged in mad vehement war.

He stood unmoved, and with experienced skill
  Prepared his ship to meet the coming gale;
E'en now resounding through the rigging, shrill—
  Tremendous straining on the belching sail;
  While rushed the seas along the weather rail
Like hoary demons thirsting for their prey;
  Though vainly yet they can her sides assail,
They rise to smite; she nimbly glides away,
And seems with those dread crests like a coquette to play.

Now grouped on deck, all hands in dumb suspense
  Watch her bold course along the watery maze,
And as they look to windward, looming thence
  Like some weird turrets through the drifting haze,
  Three lonely islets strike their wond'ring gaze;
Upon their towering cones the last red glare
  Of dying Eve sheds a portentous blaze,
As if the torch of Hell had kindled there
A triple fire to lure sad wanderers to despair.

The "Three Kings" these! infixed amid the flood,
   Like sentries grim that watch the outmost shore
Of this rude land, where oft barbaric blood
   Is made in sacrificial founts to pour;
   When the fierce shock of direful battle o'er,
The victors haste their captives to devour;
   Like ogres foul, exulting lap the gore,
And deem the feast their gods appointed dower—
Such is this race on whom a genius dark doth lower.

But who shall blame, since Nature's self doth urge
   These savage people to such horrid deeds;
'Tis her edicts that form as they diverge
   Our various states, our actions, and our creeds;
   And who can say her influence e'er misleads?
To follow Nature, is but to obey
   That potent voice which in each bosom pleads
Against all that our pleasure might bewray,
And seeks to guide us on the prime appointed way.

All men are vile! but Fate has favored some,
   And raised them o'er their less enlighten'd kind;
Yet all from the same dusty substance come,
   And all to equal follies are inclined,
   And all at last a common rest must find;
Yet earth-born favors shed upon a few,
   Affect them so, they fancy Heaven designed
Them as superior to the general crew,
When peradventure they more loathsome wiles pursue.

But hark! the gale with added fury blows,
   And wilder from their chains the waves are cast;
Still to the storm our ship her canvas shows,
   Fearful to reef until to starboard past
   Those three lone isles. Then from each shiv'ring mast
The belching sails were shortened in amain;
   Laborious task! to furl in such a blast,
Or on the yard a footing to maintain
When deep the vessel heels as ne'er to right again.

And one there was among our trusty crew,
  Who sought the lee yard arm—a dangerous post
When winds like these so energetic blew.
  He came from Candia, somewhere on the coast,
  And in his youth, as he was wont to boast,
Had served in a smart Levantine polacca;
  And oft among the Turks, his corsair host
Would single out some ship, board her and sack her,
And with unchristian gore her pitchy timbers lacker.

Antonio he was called; nor seaman's life
  Than his career had e'er so chequer'd been;
With stirring acts each vivid page was rife,
  Or tinged with hues of many a florid scene,
  Such as invest youth's morn with dazzling sheen.
In manhood's prime again he swept the seas,
  That stretch the weird Malaysian isles a-tween,
And oft as flashed his silver-glinting krees,
He gave his pirate banner to the piping breeze.

'Twas said he loved; that disappointment fell,
  With its enduring sting had smote his heart,
And made of life an ever-burning hell,
  Till all of good expired beneath the smart,
  And demons rose to play their horrid part.
He had the air of one subdued by grief—
  Of one who bore within a restless dart,
To whom no thing of earth could bring relief;
But in his lightest hours black Misery was chief.

But that was past; the blow had come and gone;
  The wound was healed, though still the scar remained;
And oft in merriest mood, some flash upon
  His soul would burst—and there awhile detained—
  Writhe with a woe intense, that lingering reigned
Like an unconquered sin; till Pride would bring
  His iron will to bear; Peace then regained
Stood fast; while Memory's envenomed sting,
Couched in her lair, prepared to make her cat-like spring.

Genius of ill! that ruthless doth awake
   The buried shadows of departed years,
And on our souls in mournful music break
   The dirges of the dead; and bid our fears
   Rise with the sound dissolved in kindred tears;
Alas! how few the joys thy pencil gilds;
   How dark the scene that in thy lune appears!
When retrospection sweeps the vanished wilds—
Her every backward glance another ruin builds!

He who hath mused until his mind became
   A boiling gulf of fierce tempestuous thought,
Where fiends disported and with tongues of flame
   Up from the deep incessant horrors brought;.
   Must by such woe—such hellish sorrow taught—
Have cursed the hour of his nativity.
   And longed for respite—respite even sought
In cold Occlusion's shadowy apathy;
For soul may keenly feel when pulse hath ceased to be.

And thus Antonio: by continuous woe
   From cheerful man into a demon turned;
His sullen breast still owned the fatal blow—
   Still for one shade his manly spirit burned,
   One lovely shade in sweet devotion urned;
And his bronze cheek was plow'd by furrow'd care,
   The signals of a love that ever yearned,
That ever felt its yearning empty air,
Till it recoiling sank a prey to grim Despair.

Withal he lived—the wretched often live—
   When happier beings find untimely tombs;
Each Fate their proper state doth rightly give—
   One suffers here—one in immortal glooms—
   As good or ill their future being dooms,
So lived Antonio; till the awful roar
   Of coming Death through his rude nature booms,
Calling his ghost to that mysterious shore,
Whence none who tread its maze can earth again explore.

High swell the winds, as up the tapering stay
   Antonio springs. Thence on the yard he goes,
O'er which in cascades huge the surges play—
   And there the flapping sail he snugly stows.
   Whilst thus employ'd, aloft the vessel rose
On a vast wave, then plunging lurched a-lee;
   The quick convulsion down Antonio throws
From his loose hold into the whelming sea,
'Gainst which he long did cope in mortal agony.

Hoarse o'er the deck the dire alarum ran,
   And far astern the rattling life-line sped—
Uncoiled in vain; swift from the drowning man
   The stooping ship in long-vibrations fled,
   And wintry beat the wave on his devoted head.
He shouted; but his shrill, ear-piercing cries
   Bay'd but the winds and filled our hearts with dread
As fixed perforce we stood; whilst from our eyes
The bubbling drops showed how we mourned the sacrifice.

'Twas done! The drama of his life was played;
   The curtain fell and all of earth had past;
The closing debt of Nature had been paid;
   The full account of his existence cast,
   And the obstructed soul was free at last.
Nor should we mourn him, or at his swift fate—
   If sudden, not untimely—stand aghast
Since once we all must pass the dreadful gate,
And to the crawling worm our temples dedicate.

White-starred Orion sinks beyond the deep,
   And calmer now the dying whirlwinds beat;
The seas decreasing gradual sink to sleep,
   And clouds disparting, still on pinions fleet
   To leeward borne, career in wild retreat—
Subsides the storm; the night revolving wanes,
   And morn awakes our weary eyes to greet;
Then o'er the void a calm unbroken reigns;—
Three days the vessel hangs, nor breath of wind obtains.

Three days wind-bound she burned beneath the sun
  That cloudless shot its fiery-natured rays;
When, as the evening shades descended dun,
  A languid breeze across the ocean plays—
  Its urging force the yielding ship obeys.
Then soon upon our beam a coast appear'd,
  Whose vernal heights awoke our loudest praise—
Whilst Expectation, every bosom cheer'd,
As tow'rd the smiling shore our wonted course we veer'd.

He who hath tost upon the restless seas
  Whilst months unvaried rolled above his head—
Dull months, surcharged with grim uncertainties,
  And all the dangerous toils the deeps bestead
  On such as may their treacherous mazes thread;
How hath he felt his pulse vibrate anew
  When slow emerging from its watery bed—
Thin as a vapor and as ether blue,
Some land's dim outline beamed auspicious to his view.

High beat our hearts as brighter morning grew,
  And dim revealed, amid the purple haze—
As silky mists aside their curtains drew—
  A lofty shore, to each expectant gaze.
  A shore with beauty clad, that might amaze
The ardent Moslem, who in feverish dreams
  Foresees that blissful land, where houries' blaze,
Sweet gardens bloom, and by clear-tinkling streams,
The faithful gently rest while Joy perpetual beams.

Such this fair land. Soon on the placid tide
  Near quiet Auckland we at anchor swing;
Anon with rapid keel the wave divide,
  As in the launch our sweeps resounding spring—
  To shoreward bent on subtle bartering.
The strand attained; out from the boat we leap
  And join a troop of savages, who bring
Barbaric objects all cast in a heap,
Which like sly Jews they vow to barter very cheap.

We met these natives several leagues north-west
  Of Auckland; on a wide and barren shore
Where spiry fern-trees waved in wild unrest,
  And rifted rocks with yellow lichens hoar
  Strew'd the sea's-margin in confusion o'er.
Whilst far south-east, a lonely mountain rose,
  Whose peak no foot had ventured to explore,
For thus the wise-men say—the legend goes—
That round its granite head a storm malignant blows.

Extending west two lofty peaks appear,
  Once horrid in volcanic energy,
But now extinct; bold, rugged, bleak and sere,
  They sullen stand in sad torpidity,
  Whilst round their craters mingled hideously
Huge scoria-blocks oppress the rocky sides,—
  Huge lava-tracks still rug the blasted lea—
Or from the ledge that land and sea divides
In shivering columns yawn above the chafing tides.

'Twas daring Tasman and his roving crew
  Who first these islands in their wanderings found;
When hither led in quest of countries new;
  Then heard one night the rolling breakers sound,
  The next at anchor lay in harbor-bound;
Upon thy cliffs Eaheianowmawe, first
  His vision glanced; yet must his teeth have ground
When thee, or Tavia Poenamoo, he burst
From his torn jaws. Lud, how the Dutchman must have curst!

But if infernal in their names, these isles
  Are by boon Nature with rich gifts endow'd
Such as few lands may boast. Yet vicious wiles
  Their copper hosts in a dark mantle cloud.
  A stalwart race are they, self-will'd and proud,
Revengeful, fierce, and as a tiger cruel;
  . Thus when a foe is caught th' inhuman crowd
Consign him to a stack of blazing fuel;
Then eat him with the gust of Scotchmen eating gruel.

Meanwhile as on the sandy beach we stood,
A runner from an ancient chieftain came
Desiring us to visit—if we would—
His kingly home, as helpless, old and lame
He lay bed-ridden—living on the fame
Won when he joy'd in manhood's vigorous prime.
Ere long we went—for commerce was our aim—
And led, began a mountain-side to climb,
Till reached a grot we saw a relic of old Time.

Dark was the grot, worn in a hollow crag
Impending from the mount's basaltic side,
Mete dwelling for some foul night-haunting hag;
Or yelling ghost, or evil thing to bide,
Or witch her spell to ply at eventide.
Blood-freezing, too, as Winter's frigid scowl.
This maori dread; where many chiefs had died;
And gave their flesh to the carnivorous fowl,
Which wheeling overhead in doleful flocks did howl.

We boldly prest into the gloomy grot,
And soon distinguish'd through the twilight shade
A withered being on a leafy cot,
By a slow fire, almost untended laid.
But one, a dark and pleasant-featur'd maid
Stood by the couch of her expiring sire;
In gleaming jad and maro white array'd,
While oft she smote a rude, canorous lyre
As if to soothe the soul so wrought with anguish dire.

But when the dusky maid ourselves beheld,
She ceas'd to play and trembled in affright,
While frequent sobs in sad succession well'd
From her lorn breast. Betimes a varying light
Glanc'd from her eyes, dark as the noon of night.
She seemed so kind, so beautiful, so good,
That the most rugged softened at the sight;
And wrapt in wonder bold Ben Nebo stood,
While warm Desire aroused the current of his blood.

Nor deem him weak within whose fiery veins
  Love's gushing torrent rolls its molten stream,
'Tis Nature's self, this wondrous law ordains,
  And charms the sense with glowing thoughts, that seem
  But the wild fancies of a heated dream.
'Tis Nature's self that cheers this lower state
  With Love's magnetic and exciting beam;
That man may feel—and feeling recreate
In pleasures which the dreams of Heaven ante-date.

But if each breast in loving tumult heaved,
  Still it was held within decorous bound,
For all were with the sad event aggrieved
  And sorrow'd for the maid in anguish drown'd;
  For men at times with humane hearts are found.
And gazing on the chief—a deep-drawn sigh
  Foretold th' event. Mad-like he glared around,
In Death's rude grasp convuls'd. Then glaz'd his eye,
The dank sweat stood upon his brow—he soon must die.

Ere long he went the ever solemn way
  That all must pass who eat of mortal food;
And as inane upon the couch he lay,
  His beauteous child with tears his brow bedew'd,
  And fragrant flowers upon his bosom strew'd.
Anon with pliant hand her harp she strung,
  And sang his praise in elegiac rude;
Sonorous forth her plaintive voice she flung,
And Echo shrill replied the answ'ring woods among.

Ben Nebo heard enrapt those ditties wild,
  As at the cavern's mouth he pensive stood
Gazing upon the maid, by love beguil'd,
  In feverish, dreamy and uncertain mood,
  As passion kindled in his glowing blood.
Yet he was not of common dust; he dealt
  Severely with the sports of Earth, pursued
By her poor parasites. Yet now he felt—
Ignoble thought! his heart in soft affection melt.

Nor proof against his love-inciting glance
  Was she—nymph of this rude volcanic glade;
Coy in her tearful eye a flash would dance
  That could alight a hermit's bosom staid,
  And oft had havoc of lorn striplings made.
Her gaze on Nebo fell, and added flame
  On his awaking love was surely laid.
His whole frame kindled. He was not the same
Now as erstwhile unto this fated place he came.

Ere long a troop of Maori's thread the cave,
  And bade the maiden hasten swift away;
For day hung trembling o'er the western wave,
  And fixed for sea their lengthy barges lay;
  Obedient to their will she ceased to play.
And sobbing left the cell; whilst all our band
  Departing, coursed the deep-descending way.
But yet afore we reached the open strand
Gray shadows stooped upon the circumambient land.

And when the sea's wide margin was attain'd—
  When sooty Night her veil incumbent spread
On flood and fell, with keen emotion pain'd,
  We found that Nebo, who had walked ahead,
  Had from the ranks most singularly fled.
The alarum given; at a halt we stood,
  Unslung our firelocks, and, with stealthy tread
Through the dark glen our restless search pursued,
And oftentimes we paused and lustily hallooed.

In vain; but Echo, from her weird recess
  Repeating, murmured to each wild halloo;
Till with misgivings none would fain express,
  We stopp'd awhile uncertain what to do;
  When from a copse near by, a whistle blew,
And instantly a shower of arrows fell
  Among our ranks. At once to arms we flew,
Pour'd forth a volley, which produced a yell
From the swart wretches. Then, we turned and crost the dell.

And on a ridge, like tigers held at bay,
　　We kept our station all that ling'ring night,
Unmoved till dawn; then formed in close array
　　We made a charge to terminate the fight—
　　We charged, and put the savages to flight;
Then as we chased the panic-stricken men,
　　Our hearts no mercy knew; but grim delight
We felt, as furious through the rugged glen
We gave them rolls of shot until they howled again.

Still Nebo came not; nor a single trace
　　Of him, far as we sought was visible.
Sudden he disappear'd, and at a place
　　Where woods of densest growth o'er-hung the fell,
　　And splinter'd chasms yawned all terrible—
Here he was lost; tho' through what cause, in vain
　　We strove to know. Still most believed the spell
That bore him hence, was that pernicious bane
Of weak-souled man—a woman—save this canting strain!

Is woman, then, a source of ill to man?
　　It cannot be! 'Twas Nature sent her here
His ills to soothe, but not his ire to fan;
　　To temper every blast that circles near;
　　To love and cheer him as a being dear.
For this she lives; and as your husband teaches,
　　Your matron follows up her part austere—
Hugs, cooks, doats, toils, and even neatly stitches
That most repulsive thing—a pair of worn out breeches.

Is woman, then, the enemy of man?
　　She who will love him so that e'en his pants—
Snip's curse upon them! pass beneath her scan,
　　And those sweet eyes that kindle at a glance
　　O'er torn limb-covers sharply look askance.
Is she his foe? She who would do all this?
　　Hear Echo answer, no! What can enhance
Man's comfort more—What so increase his bliss,
As a sweet woman who in nothing is remiss?

A truce to preaching. As the sun declin'd
  We reached our boats and o'er the chafing main
Swift-pulling sought the brig, aggrieved to find
  No sign of our lost comrade; but again
  Resolved to press no more the Maori plain,
Straitway uphove our chain; and smart the breeze
  That filled our sails. Yet as we toiled amain,
A seaman, on the beach a figure sees;
And cries vociferous rise in sounding melodies.

Our task laborious for awhile we stay'd;
  Our glasses on the stranger bring to bear,
And gladly scan through the involving shade
  Our bold Ben Nebo. Soon a lusty pair
  Of oarsmen in the gig, no labor spare
To fetch the truant to his pitchy home.
  Thence safe install'd, he told with simple air
How he from the land-rovers came to roam;
But we'll be brief, for all he said would fill a tome.

The cause of his evanishment, was this:
  That being caught in Love's pernicious snare,
He had determined—though he went to Dis—
  To seize the dusky maid—and perforce bear
  Her to the brig. Yet ere the deed he dare
Attempt, a band of Maoris plac'd amid
  A thicket sent a shower of arrows fair
A-past his ears; but the thick darkness hid
Him from their aim. He fled; and where a pyramid

Of rock arose he made a warlike stand
  Against the cruel hordes that battled round;
But when in pieces flew his shivered brand,
  Death had indeed the misadventure crown'd
  Had he in timely flight no refuge found.
Thence safe he lay conceal'd in forest close,
  Whilst serpent-like his crafty foe-men wound
Through the dark wood. At length reliev'd of foes,
He sallied from his lair and to the sea-shore goes.

But though escap'd with life, he was, in sooth,
  A man of grief—sad to the last degree—
For hopeless Love frowned on his opening youth,
  And every year increased his misery;
  But still his cup full as it seem'd to be,
Was yet to darken with a deadlier gall;
  A wilder wave must rug his angry sea;
A dismal blast descend surpassing all—
And gloomy Desolation on his bosom fall.

Avast! let Luna-smitten songsters sing
  The pangs of hopeless Love in measured state!
We, who cold-blooded are in every thing
  Are somewhat skeptic on that pensive fate—
  The ghostly vapor of a morbid pate.
If such there be—as poets represent—
  Unhappy lovers forced to separate,
And moan through dreary years with sorrow shent,
Then by the gods 'tis well when they with earth are blent!

Three weeks revolve: and now afloat again
  We sweep excursive o'er the lawless wave;
Nor aught of ill experience; nor restrain
  Our course, till Farewell, from his briny grave
  Cloud-capp'd ascends. Then rude the tempests rave;
But nautic skill prevails their fury o'er,
  And smoother seas at length our channels lave;
North-curving now we seek the broken shore,
Press through the boisterous straits and see the Cape no more.

Chain-bound we swing. Ashore the seamen leap;
  Engage in barter with a swarthy band,
Who had of native wares a motley heap,
  Such as are wrought by many a skilful hand—
  By nature taught—within this unknown land;
And they—the people—were a noble race—
  Few forms so perfect eye of limner scann'd;
Yet quaint tattoo disfigured every face,
Where untam'd Passion left its grim, repellent trace.

Uncouth the manners of these vengeful tribes—
  As polar night their minds barbaric dark;
These briefly th' untutored muse describes,
  Or rather customs worthy of remark;
  Thus, when in death a Maori lieth stark,
They think three days from thence, his heart away
  Is borne, closed in a shell of kouri bark,
By a huge angel, swift to climes that lay
Beyond the molten disk, there as a soul to stay.

Here in the midst of pleasure, quite at ease
  The hearty ghost maintains an envied state—
Alone it lives. No other ghost can tease
  Or maul, when once 't has left its fleshy weight
  Like an old chrysalis, to dessicate
On this dry earth. But in that blest abode
  All sorts of pleasures tend to elevate;
Which to enjoy, should make a man unload
Life's mighty burden, and pursue so fair a road.

And suicide, that rather doubtful act
  The stolid Maori deems a proper deed;
Nor on the couch of anguish long be rack'd,
  When from a scratch an artery can bleed,
  And his good heart from every trouble freed,
Find sweet repose in its appointed Heaven;
  But women most, who most may Heaven need,
Affect this sort of soul-exalting leaven;
And to one man self-slain of women there are seven.

For instance, 'tis a very common thing,
  For maids to whom Love's favors come amiss,
To end their mishaps by a sliding string,
  And slip their souls into eternal bliss—
  A most judicious policy is this.
Ay, even matrons who have wrought to passion
  Their loving lords, and felt a cudgel kiss
Their shoulders, have eschewed another lashin',
By cutting their dear throats. A very worthy fashion.

And quite worth copying by our christian dames;
   As then of nuptial ills there might be less,
And less of those debasing midnight games,
   That sometimes Wedlock's votaries distress,
   With pangs that celibates could ne'er depress.
For if they used the Maori's hard decree—
   That wives when flogg'd should turn to nothingness,
A horsewhip would set ill-match'd couples free,
Silence their growls—egad! and help morality.

But if from savage ethics we should scorn
   To learn, let us the fierce barbarian view
With some attention, as of fable shorn
   He stands in his primeval nature true,
   Disclosing traits that moralists may rue.
How strange the phases of our mortal race!
   How strong in all is evil shadow'd through!
How hard to deem such grovelling things the place,
The shrine, of a pure flame that time cannot efface!

But who shall judge? Perhaps in the vilest, dwells
   That which may live when planets have expired;
There is in man a monitor that tells
   Of an immortal something; but enwired
   In fleshly coils, that yield not as desired;
It lies in cryptic bars imbound, close pent
   Like a caged eagle, whose spirit fired
With thoughts exultant as for Heaven meant—
Shackled remains—a soul—with callow ashes blent.

Terrific thought! Is man a deathless thing?
   Will he exist when known no longer here?
If so, 'tis well to give up vaporing
   And trim the sails anew; nor more career
   In those fell tracks through which so many steer.
Life's but a dream—a little puppet show—
   Compared to what may be beyond the bier;
If all its years were prest into one woe,
They would not make the wise one joy of Heaven forego.

What is this world; what are its trifling joys
  To him who hears the last sad tocsin sound?
When all that's beautiful his fancy cloys,
  And his wan sight, where'er it glares around
  Sees but a hollow in the yawning ground.
How vain, how pigmy, then all earth appears,
  How dread the future deep in horrors drowned,
How much the soul the doubtful exit fears;
And anguish in each sigh foreboding Conscience hears.

Enough of this cant, theologic stuff—
  Out on the man who would his betters teach!
He merits for his pains a sound rebuff;
  For 'tis the height of impudence to preach,
  Or with rude sense the chafing rabble teach.
The wisest mind will on itself revert,
  And by experience warned, like flint, to each
Gregarian sentiment remain inert;
The dullest student thinks the wisest tutor pert.

Whilst thronged upon the shell-bespangled strand
  Our men a commerce with the blacks essay'd.
The chief Tom-a-tee-wa-kee, and a band
  Of giant guards, a first appearance made,
  Stalking in lordly pride the vernal glade.
A man of war this chief—his endless name
  Was syllabled afar. 'Twas grimly said
That when Tasman unto this island came,
He ate a whole boat's crew and made a deathless fame.

As on the beach he stood, his tawny hand
  Vain-glorious swayed a stony-headed spear;
Two anklets wrought of jad his ankles spann'd,
  And coral drops hung pendant from each ear:
  But what the timid most did strike with fear,
Were blood-red patches o'er his features smear'd,
  So that he made a figure rather queer
To contemplate; but woe to such as sneer'd,
Since in his own conceit, perfection he appeared.

Nor on his face alone vermilion glowed,
  Big rings of crimson 'bout his limbs were placed,
Whilst lurid moons in hideous glory showed
  A wavering cluster round his naked waist,
  By a light maro negligently braced.
A king he was: beneath a moa's plume
  He stood like some old god in splendor graced,
Whose glance might penetrate the farthest gloom;
Bid Nature smile serene, or funeral garbs assume.

But most he gloried in an ornament
  That kings had seldom worn upon their backs,
Save when upon the scaffold overbent;
  It was but a ship-carpenter's broad-axe
  Fit to fell spars or beat off deck attacks;
Which as a present came from Captain Cook,
  Who sent it by a dozen well-armed jacks.
The shining pledge our chief delighted took—
Then hung it from his neck to make him better look.

Meanwhile we traded; and like traders smart,
  Extoll'd our own and damn'd the Maori wares;
In short, engaged in every trading art—
  To plant our coils or scape our neighbor's snares;
  For he who in commercial matters spares,
Is a mere fool; since if our sight be true
  'Twould be as safe to thread brigandish lairs
With a fat wallet; as in business, to
Look for fair-dealing when so many like to jew.

When the Sinopean with his greasy link
  Went barking out to seek an honest man,
He must have been a little daft, to think
  That with a common flambeau, he could scan
  That creature never known since time began.
Though often sought, remaining still unknown;
  A phœnix in the great creative plan;—
A priceless gift from human bosoms flown;
Enough to make a god though held itself alone.

"An honest man's the noblest work of God":—
  So wrote that curt, incisive genius, Pope;
And, whilst accordant to its truth we nod,
  The axiom cuts into the heart of Hope,
  And Nature vainly emulates the trope.
Withal, the world survives the bitter loss,
  Or, if it feel, can with its sorrow cope.
An honest man no doubt—like gold in dross—
Might with pure lustre shine; but who would bear his cross?

To be eccentric by the mob is deemed
  A woful, or at least unseemly, sign;
An independent mind is ill esteemed,
  By oafs who never trespass on the line
  Which Fashion sets, her vassals to confine.
Hence woe to him who, in this piping age,
  Would as an "honest man" his course define—
Right soon would he in Bedlam find a cage,
Or in inch peices rent attest the public rage.

Go to, thou preacher—cease thy irksome strain!
  These dull, long-winded dissertations fly:
Resume thy prime discourse, and tell again
  How pass'd events our hardy seamen by.
  Soon as dusk Eve in shadows brooded nigh,
A maid appears! Fair is her blooming form,
  And coy the glance of her expressive eye;
Long are her locks, and red her lips, and warm
Her winning smile—'twould take the coldest heart by storm.

Clad in such charms, no wonder if this maid
  Were by our heroes very much admired;
For man is with such wanton thoughts inlaid
  That by a simple look his blood is fired,
  And Reason sinks in sodden passion mired.
Pale Virtue, then, completely put to rout,
  Retreats till Pleasure gains what Love desired;
Which, after all, is hardly worth a flout—
Venus insidious lures, then rudely turns you out.

Pernicious goddess! sent to trouble man
 With thy all-powerful—all-alluring bane;
Chief of our ills, since mother Eve began
 To long for that whose sad effect was Cain—
 Whose sad effect still haunts the human strain.
Nor with the heart alone thy mission ends;
 But at thy mercy oft our purse is lain;
And when thy worshipper his cash expends,
Cast from thy arms to rot the hapless wretch descends.

As stood the maid within an easy ken,
 Ned Bastion's eyes her buxom charms explore;
With heated blood he gazed, deep blushing, when
 Her eyes gave forth their hot, electric store,
 And conjured fancies full of love galore.
She, too, obedient to a subtle power,
 Felt weird sensations through her bosom pour;
And shivering at the lad's magnetic lower,
Shrunk like some tender plant that at the storm doth cower.

Ned saw her tremor, and like a bold tar—
 Never to war, or grog, or love averse—
Resolved to win the prize, should nothing mar
 The course he laid. So first his beaded purse
 He gave to smooth the way—ne'er a whit worse
For such fair grading. Then his wiles he plied,
 Till close-besieged Love cried for quarter; terse
Was his answer. As fell the eventide,
Afar with glowing steps he bore the willing bride.

The bull-horn'd moon above the woods arose,
 Diffusing round a pale, mysterious light,
When from an arduous search, the sailors close,
 And meditate on Bastion's sudden flight.
 Some wished to seek him even thro' the night,
But others on the project sternly frowned,
 And urged it best to wait till morn, when right
They could the wilds explore. Meanwhile profound
And dense, confluent clouds the waning orb surround.

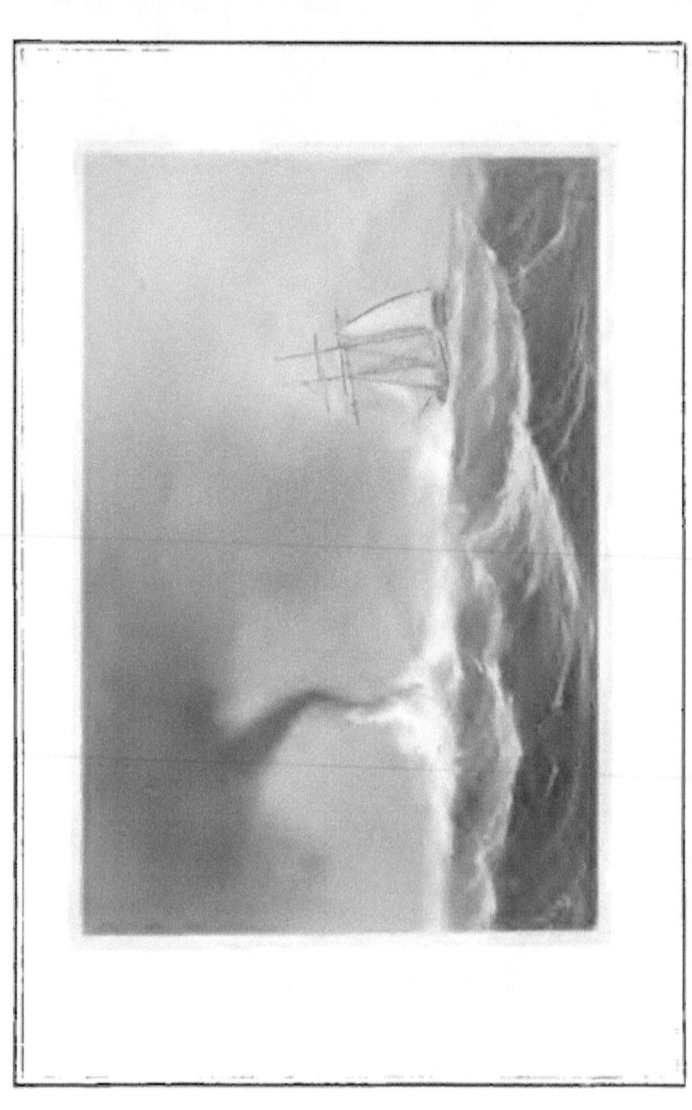

While yet they stood in doubtful council bound,
  Led by the mate, who acted as their chief,
A lengthen'd yell burst from the woods around,
  Grim-startling all. At once for fell relief
  To arms they flew; and from a neighboring reef
Stood fast—whilst arrows sped in whistling showers,
  Sore-wounding several—and one man, Tom Keef,
Death-laying on the rock. Fierce battle lowers,
Shots, yells, and imprecations fill the silvan bowers.

But such a stream of missiles on them rained,
  That they at last were driven to the beach;
And leaping in their boats, awhile sustained
  The brunt unflinching, pent within the reach
  Of the barbaric darts. At length, when each
Had half-a-dozen hideous injuries got,
  They desp'rate grew, together made a breach,
And raked the foe with fusilades of shot,
Whilst heaps of swarthy dead begrimed th' accursed spot.

Meanwhile they set the carpenter to work,
  Who of some timbers built a sturdy screen;
Behind this all the crew did closely lurk,
  And fire whene'er the crafty foes were seen
  To issue from their covert, and between
The arching trees discharge their weapons rude.
  But though our men maintain'd a dauntless mien,
The Maoris were with such fierce rage endued,
That neither vantage gained in the protracted feud.

While yet the seamen held their wav'ring state,
  A sullen boom rolled o'er the ruffled deep:
A signal from the ship, bidding the mate
  And his bold comrades from the battle keep,
  And swift unto the waiting vessel sweep.
They heed the summons: soon her pitchy walls
  Receive them from the waves that warring leap.
The windlass arm; and as the tempest falls,
Heave round the rattling coils tim'd by the clanging pauls.

The moon recedes beyond the misty west.
   And all around but foaming billows play;
Swift wing the frigate-birds in wild unrest,
   And shrieking the descending orbic bay,
    Whilst fast the trader plows her onward way.
The land is gone, no more its rocky arms
   A shelter lend, no more its shoals betray;
All, all have pass'd, and sea-born storms and calms,
And terrors unexpress'd here vent their dread alarms.

Canto II.

Ye shrill sea-breezes that so plaintive sigh
   O'er the bleak bosom of the sleepless sea:—
Sing as resounds your doleful lullaby,
   Of such as exiled from the peaceful lea,
    Feel thy sharp fangs in full severity;
In thunder tones, O ocean! roll along
   The dark, dark woe of those whom Destiny
Dooms o'er the lawless wave their course prolong—
Cærulean Neptune join, O join the mournful song!

As the free bird that cleaves the boundless air
   With nought to interrupt her forward flight,
So once again the dashing sea we dare,
   And fly exultant on the tempest's might,
    While swift astern the billow flashes white;
And sweet the joy we feel, when piping loud
   The wild wind whistles round the topmast light,
Strains the taut sail and murmurs thro' the shroud,
Whilst on the good ship flies with vibrant force endowed.

Lost was Ned Bastion. Oblivion drew
  O'er him a veil which none could penetrate;
Nor to be lifted, till with hand anew
  Upon the tablets of omniscient Fate,
  Should rise expos'd each vague, mysterious trait.
So let him rest. Nor on his errors dwell;
  Nor anxious on his doubtful end debate—
Since 'tis the same, where'er we cast the shell
When we shall cease to be, all equal slumber well.

Cook's fretful Straits have far to windward past,
  And smiling skies inspire each hopeful breast;
The course for Santelmo is set; and fast
  Before fresh aiding gales the trader prest;
  And by no ill-presaging sign distrest,
The men rejoice. To merriment give rein;
  Huge canteens flow—rude music adds its zest;
They dance, they revel, and they sing amain;
And long as storms permit their jocund sports maintain.

Ah, could we thus with lithesome folly cheer
  The cold dull round of this attritious life,
Less grim, less absolute, it might appear—
  Man less with upas attributes seem rife,
  And to exist require less bitter strife.
But no! this is a dismal place of tears,
  Where to each heart Destruction holds a knife:
He who with mirth his cup of sorrow cheers,
Like a mad clown among a troop of ghosts appears.

Who stranger is to woe? Whose breast ne'er felt
  The arrowy thought of that terrific hour
When flesh shall into mould'ring ashes melt,
  And all that lived, at Death's corrosive lower,
  Yield all its beauty, all its pomp, and power.
Who hath not trembled at the very thought,
  And felt the sweetest cup of pleasure sour,
That all he loved, lived for, and wrought,
Must feed the livid worm, and crumble into nought?

Ill boots it what our state, when earthward prone
  We hear the clarion calling us to leave
This shallow world, and enter all alone
    The mansions of the dead. How deep we grieve
    To part, for on this little scene we weave
Those fragile woofs our wonder and delight—
  Alas! so often shining to deceive.
Poor timid things! We loathe so far a flight;
Fearful if lost the way we plunge in endless night.

What riseth dimly on the briny verge
  With rugged peak ascending to the sky?
'Tis fair Santelmo, centred on the surge,
    Aloof from all the isles, that clust'ring lie
    Beneath Ascian's azure canopy.
Here like some goddess of the deep, she stands;
  Whose strength alone the tempest can defy,
Nor Ocean heed, though harsh upon her sands
He leads with sullen rein his rude, impetuous bands.

As to our gaze the island plainer grew,
  A hideous spectre caught each startled eye;
By whirlwinds urged across the deep, it blew
    Till on our beam it foaming thundered by;
    Alarmed we saw the watery spire draw nigh,
And steer almost athwart the traders' course;
  While round the billows heave, and upward fly,
Till one huge jet revolves with lightning force:
Loud howl the curling winds; seas raging bellow hoarse.

Our gunner comes: the starboard guns are primed,
  Their muzzles on the watery column bear;
Quick as the vessel lurched—by order timed—
    The linstocks on the nitrous priming flare;
    One loud concussion rends the trembling air.
Re-echoing ocean murmurs to the roar
  Deep as the lion thunders, when his lair
Invasive feels the foe. Down-crashing pour
The broken torrents vast; and lo! the peril's o'er!

The transient deluge past; our course again
  For Santelmo's uprising shores we held;
When, as the glaring day began to wane,
  O'er a long shelf where high the breakers swell'd;
  Into a landlocked cove the brig impell'd;
Here laid secure, we swing at anchor bound
  Amid a scene whose weird enchantment spell'd
Our souls as with a talisman; around
Romantic prospects rose with nemorous beauties crowned.

Soon as the crimson beams of daylight rose,
  Away to land our men for water rowed;
Moor near a fount, whose crystal current flows
  Low-bickering down a ledge. The casks they load,
  And strong-lashed, in appointed order stowed.
This done, in dalliance for awhile on shore
  They roam excursive. As along they strode,
With wistful eyes they scan the landscape o'er,
And muse on scenes whose like none e'er beheld before.

Scenes bright as visions of that beauteous home.
  Islam's great Prophet promiseth the blest;
Led by sweet houries, ever pleased, they roam
  Through fairy regions of enchanted rest,
  Where suns are clear; fields alway vernal drest;
Woods thick with leaves; and flowery all the dales,
  Where brooklets wind; and o'er the lakelet's breast
The sacred bird in tuneful joyance sails,
And beats with flapping wing the spicy-laden gales.

Here in this isle a dreamy beauty reigned;
  Soft overhead the fleecy clouds appeared;
Harmonious warblers in the woods maintained
  A joyous chorus that diffusive cheered—
  Our seamen wondering at the music weird.
Delicious languor, too, her elfin woof
  Spread o'er the lands. Romance each spot endear'd;
Still unimprest by man's destructive hoof,
All-glorious Nature bloomed from human wiles aloof.

Here the wild bee pursued its droning flight,
  Industrious plunderer of the honeyed flowers;
And chiming through the long moon-shining night
  Sad campanero tolled the waning hours;
  Or, sealed amid the deep umbrageous bowers,
Her dual note the lonely cuckoo plays;
  Whilst—keen presager of approaching showers—
The restless heron flutters through the maze,
Or, from some blasted tree th' aerial tumult bays.

Eld trees arise: grim druids of the wood,
  Long since beshorn of their prime loveliness,
Solemn they frown upon the solitude;
  Whilst younger monarchs tenderly caress
  Their gay companions, and with pomp impress
The neighboring scenery. Ten thousand dyes
  Imprint the glebe; and in each green recess
Sun-colored fruits the dazzled eye surprise,
And the prospective still in varied beauty vies.

Prime over all the Artocarpus reigns—
  Majestic monarch of the torrid zone—
From whose all-generous and prolific veins,
  As winds among his topmost branches moan,
  The goodly bread-fruit is spontaneous thrown.
Tree of the countless isles! Thou beauteous thing—
  Thou life dispenser; what could e'er atone
The loss of thee? whence blessings constant spring;
Nature's auspicious gift, Ascian muses sing!

Ascia's dusky race thy fruit maintains;
  Thy bark a shelter offers from the heat;
From thy light wood the swift canoe obtains;
  As plates thy leaves support the frugal treat;
  And from thy pores glutinous juices sweet
Distilled, the pangs of fiery thirst abate;
  Or lime exude to snare th' ortolans feet;
No part of thee is waste. Benignant Fate,
Thee into being called sharp misery to rebate.

Whilst gazing on the varied prospect round,
  On a tall hummock the bold seamen stood,
And saw immured in shady groves profound,
  A hamlet just obtruding through the wood—
  Sole sign of man in this deep solitude.
Fired at the sight; all caution cast aside;
  And vowed with many an exclamation rude,
That if the chief should not averse decide,
To reach the village ere descent of eventide.

Permission given, at once they haste away,
  Led by the mate, and well supplied with arms;
When, just as shut the drooping lid of day,
  Their van vociferous the watch alarms;
  Men sought their spears, and maids conceal'd their charms.
But mauger all; they marched into the town—
  A pretty place o'ergrown by waving palms;
When soon they met a native with a crown;
He was a king they found—else they had knocked him down.

Soon as he saw them, his sardonic mien
  Vouchsafed to wrinkle with an ugly smile;
He turned and led them to an arbor green,
  Where he was wont his liesure to beguile,
  And toy with maidens loveliest of the isle;
Thence he produced a most substantial cheer;
  Flesh, herbs and fruit, and fish aglow in oil;
And bade them eat, nor aught of evil fear;
For he by Nature was a generous cavalier.

Withal they longed for an inspiring taste
  Of crystal whisky or brown-colored rum;
Either of which when ardently embraced,
  Will act the part of a funereal drum,
  And tap a man head-first to regions glum.
They had no grog. To ease this want severe,
  Old cocoa-toddy served their wits to numb—
And so 'twixt many an oath, and many a leer,
They swore their host was quite a royal grenadier.

Nor stopt his bounty here. It farther spread,
  And joys provided of a fairer kind;
His guests into a spacious hut he led,
  And to each tar a buxom girl assigned,
  In whom a Pasha might new pleasure find;
And when like doves the wanton throngs were paired;
  He bade a fluter raise the sounding-wind,
Whereat each maid her agile figure bared,
And with our fervid men in mazy dancing shared.

Bismillah! 'twould astound a sultan's eyes
  To see those dark girls in that amorous dance;
As each coy maid her toil enslaving plies,
  Her lover's native ardor to enchance
  And steep his soul in Passion's molten trance;
Whilst as she swept in graceful circles round,
  Desires' hot wishes flashed in every glance,
And firing at each warm, bewildering bound,
Longed in fruition's dreams to find those wishes crowned.

Out on the dance! it is the vilest thing
  The cloven-footed genius ever brought
Into this world; virtue to loose, and fling
  Light-headed souls, by rapid motion caught,
  Into the gulf—or better, into naught.
Out on the dance! 'Tis in the giddy reel
  The plastic virgin Love's delights is taught;
When made the pressing hand betimes to feel,
Her bosom throbs with thoughts 'twere safer to conceal.

Forbear! These natives are a comely race—
  True sons of Anak, as their stature quite
O'er-topt our tallest lad—Alonzo Brace,
  A Portuguese, above six feet in hight;
  And all in strength display'd enormous might.
Unclad the men; the younger women, though
  Less careless, hide their graces from the sight
By flaxen aprons, yet contrive to show
Enough of charms, whose like few pale-faced maidens know.

Both sexes use tattoo; dye their teeth black;
 And every man has several lusty wives,
Whom he as serfs compels the grain to stack,
 Hew wood, draw water, edge his flinty knives,
 Rear children, cook, and first the honey'd hives
Bare-faced attack. Whilst he as master oft
 Loud-roaring to her task the woman drives;
Thus by hard usage she becomes quite soft,
And humbled never bears a haughty port aloft.

The native king was quite an ancient man,
 With power despotic vested in his will;
The isle was his; and since his reign began
 He had contrived with very little skill,
 One half of his unhappy race to kill.
But he was king; and kings, though common dust,
 Would lower be unless they loved to spill
Blood by the hogshead. However, Fate is just,
And kingly souls from Heaven may old Saint Peter thrust.

He had a daughter with great beauty rife—
 No lovelier damsel e'er was ushered in,
(To lead an easy sort of useless life)
 In this round world of wretchedness and sin—
 Of doubtful virtue and distempered gin.
Lithe was her form in dusky charms array'd,
 And fit her glance the coldest heart to win,
For Love's delicious wiles by Nature made,
She reigned the queen of hearts o'er all this sea-girt glade.

But sealed within her breast there was a pang
 That told of feverish wishes unsubdued—
Of sleepless thoughts, whose adder-venomed fang
 Wounds deepest in the hour of solitude,
 Nor fails to lance in the convivial mood.
Soul-piercing dreams that fated mortals speed
 To graves unripe. With such life's road is strewed;
Our steps along these hopeless ruins lead—
Ruins by sad affection ever doomed to bleed.

O Love! what is thy genius, that thou must
  With anguish wring the too-confiding heart?
Pursue with terror till he turn to dust
  The hapless wretch destined to feel the dart;
  Yet, yet delay the soul from flesh to part!
Thou fatal archer! Tyrant of our race,
  Ordained to smite with never-healing smart,
And in our breast a beauteous image place,
Which if in youth's prime fixed no other can efface.

Supreme thy power; yet, but a sacred few
  Feel its effect through long and ling'ring years;
Whose souls are tempered in a furnace, true—
  Whose hearts are pure—whom misery bathes in tears.
  These, these thy ruthless brand delighted sears;
These thy delight to fill with sharp unrest—
  Unrest increasing as the sand careers;
Till, last dread refuge of the grief opprest,
The gloomy grave extends its cold sequestered breast.   ·

In vain earth's shallow joys to him atone
  Who mourns the loss of a congenial love;
He in relentless pathos stands alone,
  Like some lorn tree, that singled from the grove—
  Smote by th' electric fury from above,
Changed by the shock, becomes a ruined spar.
  All cheerful beauties from its nature drove,
Sad droops its rifted head, and every scar
Pernicious speaks its fate and heralds it afar.

Enough, enough, forbear so dull a theme,
  The dark chimera of disordered brains;
'Tis sickly kinds that of affection dream;
  Or think its bands composed of iron chains.
  Love is but Passion, changing as the vanes
That restless wander to the veering winds;
  A moment in one heart perchance remains—
Then with frail bonds another victim binds;
'Tis like true Virtue which no searcher ever finds.

It chanced there was among the crew, a youth
Who from Tasmania as a sea-boy came;
His sire had been a ranger, and in sooth,
Upon a scaffold tumbled out in shame,
Leaving to prison writs a doubtful fame.
He was a Maltese—Jack Ispara called—
And like his honored sire was counted game;
At least his spirit never could be thralled:
He beat the boatswain thrice—and once the skipper mauled.

Jack had a lion heart; yet he was famed
For his success in acts of gallantry;
Acts so profound, Don Juan would have shamed
Had he e'er lived to hear their strategy,
Or to behold the youth's pomposity.
But let these pass; to prudes they might appear
As spiced with something of coarse ribaldry—
And we are moral too; Jack—it was queer—
Would charm the dullest girl by one good sidelong leer.

May the good Virgin save all virtuous maids
From such dread men and from their looks oblique:
But most from their embrace, which so degrades
All that is lovely in the sex, so meek—
The sex by vulgar error reckoned weak.
May all the angels—if indeed, there's any—
Preserve their lower sisters, when men seek
To blast their characters, of which there's many,
Nor deem a moral man no better than a zany.

Jack saw the gentle maid: "Aha!" quoth he,
(As on her charms his eye admiring shone),
"This buxom maiden is a prize for me;
No arms but mine so fair a form shall own—
My lips her cheek impress and mine alone,"
He said: then sprang his amorous arts to wield—
Sighed as he gazed and spoke in piteous tone,
When soon the god of hearts this truth reveal'd:
That woman close-besieged must to the sieger yield.

Love knit their hearts: he stoopt to Beauty's charms,
  She blooming youth in modest zeal desir'd;
Love's magnet lured to warm congenial arms,
  And Hymen's torch voluptuous wishes fired—
  Such the keen joys affection fond inspir'd.
Ispara, in the sweet enchantment bound,
  With his beloved into the isle retired,
And wandering where no trace could e'er be found,
In secret hid. Success their resolution crowned.

Our commerce ended: to the seas once more
  We give our lives and our storm-beaten bark;
While sinks astern Santelmo's azure shore,
  And rolling clouds arise in squadrons dark.
  Winds still are mute; but lo! afar, we mark
A sable cloud upon the purple sky
  Advancing towr'd the vertic. And soon, hark!
That melancholy sough—th' presaging sigh
Of howling winds that rack the starless canopy.

Adieu ye scenes of sweet arcadian bliss,
  That to our eyes your varied beauties spread;
How fair the contrast to a scene like this
  Where jarring tempests rouse the watery bed
  And beat inclement on the wanderer's head.
Hoarse-sounding from the hyperborean pole
  The windy gods across the billows tread;
Jove's thund'ring bolts along the concave roll,
And the terrific scene with horror fills the soul.

And fast before the wild, pursuing waves,
  Like a winged thing the shivering vessel flew;
Whilst, as with force increased the tempest raves,
  Green fear glowers on the pale, despairing crew,
  Who sick at heart their doleful station rue.
But Fate at length, with milder aspect frowned;
  Fixed to a point the hoarse tornado blew;
North-west-by-west we scoured the bleak profound;
Three weary weeks elapse and terrors still confound.

Low did she stoop among those boiling seas,
 Whilst every joint rang out its sad refrain,
As if with voice endowed, its miseries
 To chant unto the rude, tumultuous main,
 On which full many a heart had toiled in vain,
As roared the billows in malignant glee;
 And many a tender heart had mused amain
When the shrill night-winds, driving o'er the lea
Have piped around the home of him who plowed the sea.

At length the blust'ring winds began to lull—
 The seas to sleep—the clouds to break away;
And the awaking sun, emerging full,
 Gave cheering promise of a calmer day,
 And roused our spirits with his smiling ray.
Again the long imprisoned sails are spread,
 Whilst aiding gales in strains alluring play;
Nor more the wind-god's hellish wrath we dread;
Peace gilds the shining wave; the long, long storm has fled.

"A sail, a sail!" the watch sonorous cries,
 And at the cry all hands expectant gaze;
"A sail, a sail," the master's voice replies,
 As through his glass he sweeps the distant haze,
 And with attention a dim speck surveys;
Soon round the deck the sad announcement goes,
 And every face emotion dark betrays;
She is a proa—fellest of the foes—
Who in these lonely seas commercial barks oppose.

And now she squares the rising gale before,
 Fresh canvas spreads and for our vessel steers;
Whilst from each port the long resounding oar
 Aglow with foam in serried file appears,
 And cannon loom above in frowning tiers.
As the swift vulture on its quarry flies,
 So to her prey the fierce Sumatran veers;
Till fancy seems to hear th' exultant cries
That crown the triumph of her darkling enterprise.

No season this for craven-like delay,
  For fast the corsair draws within the range
Of her bow guns. At once to bear away
  The orders' given; anew our course we change,
  And north-west scud for Fijiian waters strange.
Three hours we fly; when lo, a jet of smoke
  Springs from the proa's head, and poor Will Stange,
Falls bleeding to the deck; his shoulder broke
By a huge splint rent from the counter's solid oak.

The fearful spectacle our vengeance woke,
  And swift a-port the carronades we ran;
Then as the proa cleared her smoky cloak
  We luffed, and sudden thro' her teeming van
  A broadside pour'd. And now the fight began
In real earnest. Shots incessant stream;
  Small arms resound; and louder o'er the span
Great cannon roar; anon a piercing scream
Foretold some wretch had closed lifes' miserable dream.

But fate is everything. A plunging shot
  From out the proa's forward chaser sped;
It struck the mainmast; from the riven spot
  A splinter issued; one sailor dead,
  Another wounded on the deck it spread.
These to the sick-bay we at once convey'd,
  Clear'd off the wreck, the mainmast's tottering head
With sturdy tackle in position stay'd,
Then to the brunt of war like bold tarpaulins laid.

Unbent the contest till the veil of night
  In deepest shade the grim combatants hid,
Then ceased contention; though the gory fight
  Might yet begin when morning's waking lid,
  Diffusing lustre, should the hostile bid
To arms. But as auspicious winds prevailed
  And darkness favored, we resolved to rid
Ourselves of the Malay. Away we sailed,
And many leagues had crost ere Heaven's beacons paled.

As sunk in light Bootes silvery car,
   And from the vertic fled the Northern Wain,
We gazed across the heaving deep afar,
   But saw no proa ply the chase amain
   All-furious bent the battle to maintain;
Clear were the seas, far as we questioned, clear;
   Pleased at the sight our courage we regain;
And urged tow'rd Fijiian Isles three days career—
When lo! what mystic coasts upon our lee appear!

His chart the master scans, but scans in vain,
   Whilst dark suspicions o'er his senses creep;
No isle here marks the hydrographic plane,
   Unsounded billows here unbroken sweep;
   Still as he looked upon the frowning steep.
In full relief against the azure thrown,
   With quicker force his throbbing pulses leap,
And added lustre in his vision shone;
He first had found this land, unto the world unknown!

He slyly laughed, and when his sextant showed
   The true location of this nameless isle,
He almost seemed to feel Fame's crushing load
   Upon his shoulders press, in such fine style
   That he ranked far above the common file.
For he, like humans all, was soft on fame,
   And to be famous would as lief exile
The few poor virtues which adorn a name,
Or raise man o'er the brute, by instinct much the same.

Oh for a voice like some gruff auctioneer,
   To curse the mischiefs that proceed from fame;
Which like another Eve, has settled here
   To spread awide the scathing blast of shame,
   And Satan's larders fill with human game.
Of all the ills in life's portentous list,
   Fame is the worst. She is an artful dame,
Who pouts her lips but rarely can be kiss'd,
And when within our grasp most suddenly is miss'd.

She is a jilt—the deuce to every heart,
  A queen with every wicked fancy fraught;
Withal admired, and lured by every art;
  Since few desire to be accounted nought,
  Or die without one battle being fought;
For men are fond of rising—like good leaven—
  More bent on teaching than on being taught;
Still, where one floats, of sinker's there are seven;
And after all there's doubt if this one gets to Heaven.

And man's a pompous creature; like a crane,
  Though placed on earth he lifts his head on high,
And often soars above his low domain,
  As if his nature was to upward fly
  And in remoteness dodge the sharpest eye.
Vain fool! however far he chance to soar,
  His clumsy shape the dullest sight can spy,
And though gay plumes his carcass cover o'er,
'Tis but a man beneath—a paltry man—no more.

"Fame is a rose upon a dead man's breast"—
  So saith the proverb—but, my lad, belay;
This tiresome canting now should surely rest;
  Preaching is folly when it fails to pay—
  So quoth the canters-of the present day;
And taking their advice, our moral strain,
  Like a coiled halser, shall in storage lay
Until the spirit moves us, when again
We may resume our theme and sermonize—in vain.

Ben Nebo stood upon the deck, as Eve,
  Deep-blushing, gleamed across the purple surge;
And pensive, saw the ruddy glimmer leave
  The western skies, and glowering o'er the verge
  Slow-paced to Night's engulfing void emerge;
He heard the billow's sob, the mews' shrill cry,
  The fitful zephyrs melancholy dirge,
Till Thought awaking, with a deep-drawn sigh
Joined the sad chorus with her plaintive lullaby.

What cometh from the gloomy realms of death,
　　With graceful step and form of fairest mold?
Whilst soft as summer winds expiring breath—
　　As bells that tinkle from some distant fold,
　　Or music from some seraph harpist roll'd,
Her voice melodious steals. Ben Nebo wakes,
　　And shudders at the beauteous phantom cold,
Whose glance the frozen seal of memory breaks,
And bids him breathe anew, while Hope expectant quakes.

"Ye moaning billows chant of Nora, dead—
　　Nora who perished in the bloom of youth!
Ye sea-winds wail so fair a spirit fled!
　　Ye mermaids sing the desolating truth!
　　And you ye dolphins hoarsely groan in ruth
Of her whose exit all my being wrings—
　　Discourse of Nora! Left forlorn, in sooth
No joy to me a gleam of pleasure brings,
But melting dirges Love in chime funereal rings.

"Her beauteous form is now insensate dust;
　　Long years of anguish prove her exit true;
And I have felt upon my heart the rust,
　　The blight, the canker, of a grief which few
　　Have felt tho' lives of sorrow passing through.
And since the hour that gave her to the tomb,
　　This weary pilgrimage I've learned to rue;
Yet Fate forbids an issuance from the gloom,
Till th' appointed blow completes my ling'ring doom.

"Fair Nora sleeps! her sweet voice now is mute,
　　No more its cadence can my senses please;
Her palsied hand no more awakes the lute,
　　No more her lips in ringing symphonies
　　Of Love—sad Love—resound the elegies.
Her woodland pets their darling mistress mourn,
　　But Time their grief oblivious shall appease,
Whilst I, less favored, wailing still forlorn,
Of hapless Nora chant, untimely from me torn.

"For her no more the wreathy crown I twine
   As when we roamed in days to memory dear;
For her no more enweave the fragrant vine,
   Or lure the minnow from the streamlet clear.
   Still, still of her I sing in strain austere,
As fits the dismal tenor of my soul;
   And oft methinks her spirit hovers near;
Her elfin dirges with my moanings roll;
O beauteous shade awake and with my grief condole!

"I then might know what I shall never know,
   A gleam of bliss these shadows to dispel,
And lifting up the weight of crushing woe,
   Make life appear less a terrestrial hell,
   Where Pleasures rarely flit—where Sorrows dwell;
I then might be what I was in time past—
   A firm believer in the flimsy spell,
That man was in a sacred image cast—
Which like all things of earth, experience proves——'avast"!

The loud-voiced boatswain cries, as crawling aft,
   Some order to a forward tar he gave,
Who with a gang was taking in the gaft.
   Soon as his tones rang o'er the sounding wave,
   Ben Nebo's plaints found a remorseless grave;
As up he sprang, shook off his dreams, and stood
   Like one resolved such evil wraiths to brave,
Or crush at once the ghastly-natured brood,
That with relentless scowl accurst his solitude.

Shrill blew the winds and fast our keel impell'd
   Into a placid and majestic bay;
Green woods upon the heights adjacent swell'd,
   Where cawing birds in various plumage gay
   Reshot the lustre of th' meridian ray.
Far as the eye could range, new prospects rose;
   Hills roll on hills and mountains Heav'n survey;
Soft on the strand the deep meand'ring flows,
And Nature's added charms a perfect scene compose.

And here no sign of human life was seen;
  No rural hamlet peeped between the wood,
No lonely hut appear'd upon the green,
  No vocal murmurs from the savage brood,
  Broke the dead silence of the solitude.
Far as the vision swept—'twas barren all
  A place where Nature reign'd unrivall'd rude,
Where Beauty made her gorgeous capital,
And the curs'd foot of man was never heard to fall.

The sea, the sea! once more we plow the sea,
  Loud pipe the winds that curl the onward wave;
The sea, the sea! its billows fierce and free
  Are terrors to the dull luxurious slave,
  Whose heart revolts when roaring breezes rave.
The sea, the sea! we love its rushing foam—
  And whistling gales and flowing canvas crave;
Let timid landsmen vaunt their anchor'd home—
Be ours the better fate—the boundless seas to roam.

Such the glad thoughts that every bosom held
  As o'er the yesty surge we gaily sail'd;
Yet oft Ben Nebo's feverish soul rebell'd—
  Oft his long exile from his land he wail'd—
  Oft in deep grief relentless Fate assail'd.
And thus one night, as thro' the etherial blue,
  The glistering signs his awe-struck sight regal'd,
With restless step he paced the watches through,
And pensive dreamed as they on noiseless pinions flew.

And thus he mused: "Twas in the waning year
  When sereing leaves presaged their coming doom;
When wintry blasts deep-sounding blew severe
  And crushed the flow'ret in its tardy bloom,
  That much-lov'd Nora sank into the tomb.
I still can see that pale, angelic brow—
  That lovely face a paler hue assume;
Death's rugged coulter those sweet features plow—
That dark eye dim—all—all appear before me now.

"And thou art dead! say, shall I e'er again
  Behold thee as thou wert in hours before
The icy hand of Death had on thee lain?
  I know not. Who can pierce the jealous door
  That 'gainst us shuts the Future's mystic store?
I know not—yet illusive wish would gild
  The vision, and upon my senses pour
A train of thought with this dear fancy fill'd;
But grisled doubt succeeds and frozen hope lies still'd.

"And I have loved!" Aloud the steersman here
  Broke in upon the muser's reverie:—
Quoth he: "What light is that so red, yet clear,
  Whose lustre radiates the western sea,
  And tints the stooping vapors luridly?"
Ben Nebo gazed across the sullen gloom
  To where a flickering glare upon the lee
Bespoke some ship a-fire. A hollow boom
Remurmuring o'er the deep, confirmed the fancied doom.

"A ship on fire!" the up-roused seamen cry,
  As curious to the leeward rail they run;
Anon to indicate assistance nigh—
  So wills the chief—discharge a signal gun;
  And scarce the simple task is fully done,
Ere from the light there comes another roar;
  A minute gun—we fire a second one
In hoarse reply. But as we heard no more,
Braced on the wind and tow'rd the hapless vessel bore.

It was a grand—a truly solemn sight—
  The burning of that ship upon the main;
Afar there shone a glare of ruddy light,
  As if Avernus bursting through its chain
  Had spill'd its horrors on the watery plain;
But as we gazed the rueful scene upon,
  A train of meteors lit the skies amain;
Flames, sparks, and smoke, commingled hurtling on,
Shook the dank void and glared a new Phlegethon.

And then a sound like the last trumpet, loud,
  Hoarse and terrific, roared along the waste;
And high above a black revolving cloud
  Through the abyss its nitrous volume trac'd
  Like some gigantic pall in ether plac'd,
Then as the fiery ruins downward fell,
  Diffusive, in effulgent armor cased;
The roar disparting died across the swell,
And silence over all resumed her torpid spell.

'Twas done! the wreck in countless atoms torn,
  Evanished from our deeply-wondering gaze;
So the ill-fated wretch by woes o'er borne,
  Ends at a stroke his sorrow-laden days,
  And in one last o'erwhelming ruin lays.
Such is the stern, unswerving law of Fate—
  The smallest principle that law obeys;
Man least of all that edict can rebate,
It guides the very will that seeks oblivion's state.

Oblivion! what a mystic word is thine!
  Thou opiate of all sublunary things;
Thy wraith in Death's twin-sister we divine
  Congenial balm of spirit-wounding stings,
  Whose poppy draught narcotic languor brings.
Grateful we sip; but ah! we wake again,
  And shackless Thought like a hyena springs
Intent to rend. He clanks his riven chain;
Sharp-cutting, wounds our peace and riots in our pain.

Let such as in Voltarian dreams delight,
  Draw solace from their cold philosophy;
Believe that Death is but enduring night,
  That soul dissolves when sense hath ceas'd to be—
  That life is but magnetic energy.
Let such believe—believe thus if they can;
  He must renounce such callow sophistry
Who taught the inmost shades of thought to scan,
Hath felt that subtle fire which shone ere earth began.

Can genius die? Go ask the glorious shades
　　Of the Immortals, who on Nature's page
Graved in a character that never fades
　　Their mighty glories to remotest age.
Can Manfred die—or th' Avonian sage
In stony crypt forever sleep unknown?
　　How vain to ask. 'Gainst these the cycles wage
Unequal war. Like gods they stand alone—
Like gods they make a sure eternity their own.

What matter if the outer husk decay,
　　If the inherent germ existeth still;
Or, if the spirit of the germ shall stay
　　Forever quickened and forever thrill
Innumerous spirits to its sovereign will.
Such the grand fate of earth's illustrious men,
　　Whose god-like souls distill'd such thoughts as fill
The eternal years, and with a molten pen
Imprest congenial minds until they glowed again.

What mote appeareth on the distant tide
　　As Dawn emerges from her rosy bed?
What mote that draws the lookout's glance aside,
　　As perched upon the foremast's dizzy head,
He quests to ken what ocean may bestead?
"A boat! a boat!" he hails the watch on deck;
　　Soon thro' the ship the news is trumpeted,
And the long glass is levell'd on the speck:
It is, it is a boat—a relic of the wreck!

Long was the tug across th' opposing seas,
　　And slow that boat upon the vessel drew;
At length an end to all uncertainties
　　Appear'd as Solus wheeled the vertic through,
When to our deck we hauled the wearied crew;
And when refreshing cheer their wants supplied,
　　They told their story—one that all might rue—
How took the ship a-fire—and how they tried
To still the angry flames, whose rage their power defied.

She was a Lusian ship from Lima, bound
    For Lisbon, with a load of silver ore;
When three days out a fierce tornado frown'd,
    And forced to scud at its wild mercy, bore
    South-west by-south for Pitcairn's lonely shore.
Amid the tempest—in alarm they hear
    The ship's on fire! At once the hold explore,
Where fangs of flame in hideous wrath appear—
And aftward trend, seen first within the cable tier.

In vain they toiled to quench the raging fires,
    That swept devouring through the crumbling shell;
The flames increase; soon wearied strength expires,
    And Fate on every billow seems to swell.
    Then mad for life unto the guns they fell,
And rolled afar their hoarse funereal notes,
    Such as in minute guns alone may dwell;
Nor long these spoke. Replied our brazen throats;
Told of assistance near—and urged to launch their boats.

But as the billows ran extremely high,
    One boat was in the act of launching staved,
And eighteen souls with one united cry
    Sank in the flood; but three its fury braved,
    And nearly drown'd were by the pinnace saved.
Just then her people heard our cannon sound,
    And stood away for succor; but so raved
The waters, that high noon was blazing round,
Ere on the trader's deck, a resting place they found.

And one there was among that fated train,
    Whom Memory oft in hue primeval shows,
When dreaming o'er those faded scenes, again
    Some picture in vivific beauty glows;
    Celestia! thou destined to many woes,
Torn from thy love—an exile on the deep;
    Till kindly Fate resolved thy toils to close;
And where Papuan seas cerulean creep,
On couch of coral laid thy beauteous shell may sleep.

Yet why recall a melancholy theme
  Long since in dumb negation cast away?
'Tis futile o'er departed scenes to dream,
  Or the sad past in pensive grief survey.
  The present is not one unclouded day—
But actual sorrows claim our constant care,
  And various terrors line our devious way;
Ideal anguish fades—dissolves to air,
Beside the darker shapes that haunt us everywhere.

Most sullen of the pangs that sully life—
  Grief gloomy hydra lurks in every heart;
Ceaseless until the soul-dissevering knife
  Gives its last keen—its last destructive smart—
  And bids the spirit from its temple start.
Man here was made to mourn—'tis Fate's decree—
  And he who suffers most can best depart,
Can best resign these scenes of misery,
Can best take the dread leap into eternity.

Yet life's a farce, though haply some may cry:
  Life is no farce—it is a tragedy,
Where each wan actor as he passeth by
  Howls out a lengthen'd note of misery,
  And shivering dreads his frail mortality.
A farce hath merriment—in life there's none;
  'Tis one long woe—devoid of pleasantry—
From man's first wail until his task be done
'Tis one continual strife; best closed when first begun.

Still, life's a farce. Allow that there is ill
  In many things that to this state befall;
Yet if gauged at their real worth, we will
  Discover that the hugest of them all
  Into the merest dwarfs of trouble fall.
Deaths, disappointments, pangs and penalties,
  Are ills indeed—but ills so very small
That it is strange they should disturb the ease
Of reasoning beings versed in stern philosophies.

To thoughtful men existence is a farce—
    A play composed of hollow vagaries
In which the players all one censor pass,
    And fly like chaff before the wintry breeze
    Into Eternity's unfathomed seas.
All is unreal, heartless, and unsound—
    Virtue and man unyielding enemies;
The greatest ass is oft with honors crown'd,
And plaudits greet the knave whose limbs no fetters bound.

Canto III.

The toils of seamen, rulers of the waves,
    Twice and again we celebrate in song;
Ye manly hearts! who, when hoarse Neptune raves
    And Boreas howls, excursive scud along,
    Proud of the blast—as merciful as strong!
Sons of the surge! where'er the whirlpools hiss—
    In storm-defying ships—a fearless throng
On danger's edge you ride! What courage this?
What voice can sing your deeds, ye rovers of th' abyss?

But lo! emergent from the gleaming deep—
    Serenely fair, in hues prismatic drest—
Tahitian shores along the starboard creep.
    Long-wished for haven of auspicious rest—
    A glistening gem on ocean's azure breast
Art thou, sweet isle. Hope skims the rolling tide
    With joyful wing to seek thy woody nest,
And taste those joys already dim descried—
Utopian joys, where every sense is gratified.

But soon, alas! these dreams illusive flee,
   And terror drapes th' extended prospect round;
For now alarming signs that storms decree
   Our anxious eyes with woeful glare astound;
   Three mighty zones the sickly moon surround,
O'er the North Star a blackening haze appears,
   While oft across the heaven's dark profound,
A lurid spark in rapid flight careers;
Anon indignant Jove hurls his electric spears.

Swift, too, the silver in the glassy spire
   Shrinks with the pressure of th' aerial weight;
Mysterious agent! fraught with seer-like fire
   Ether's incessant change to ante-date,
   And half the seaman's doubtful dread abate.
Still lower shrunk the boding mercury,
   Breaking the spell of leisure enervate;
All hands are rous'd—all now alert must be,
For hark, the blust'ring winds now curl the jarring sea!

North-east-by-east the blasts converging blew,
   And fast the brig before their fury sped;
Till dark above the murky verge, anew
   A mighty cliff uplifts its beetling head,
   And o'er the crew presaging terrors shed;
For futile now to clear the threat'ning edge,
   By naked masts whence every sail has fled;
Yet none despair; we may not round the ledge,
But on the beach escape the sea's engulfing dredge.

In this distress, while horror froze our blood,
   Instant elapsed all thought of danger past;
For to each eye, above the angry flood,
   Of every peril we beheld the last.
   Already Fancy sees us shipwreck'd, cast
Torn, dumb, and bleeding from the raging waves;
   Or seaward urged, in hopeless fear aghast
Sank in the stifling surge to nameless graves,
Where the voracious newt his hideous banquet craves.

Stars of the storm! twin brothers placed on high,
  Who erst were saviors of storm-beaten crews,
Say, now, where is thy aid? Loud, loud we cry,
  Bright pair! thy sea-composing bands to loose,
  Nor more resistless winds awide diffuse.
In vain, in vain—as merciless and bleak
  As the hail-volley cold—ye glint obtuse,
Whilst coastward drives the wreck; soon its huge beak
Grates on the snapping rock, and wild the drowning shriek.

The waves where'er they list, the ruins urge
  Fierce-crashing as they smite the flinty coast;
Amid them, drove before the howling surge,
  Ben Nebo shoreward hastes. Of all the host
  He and the mate but scaped th' infernal ghost,
And shivering issued from the yawning seas;
  The rest were lost; they and their floating boast
Found a release from all calamities,
And as a holocaust did Neptune's wrath appease.

Prone on the beach the dumb survivors lay,
  Left as they fell by the retreating wave,
'Till life relit its frail and fluttering ray
  Just glimmering on the margin of the grave,
  And to their shells again the spirit gave.
Then Nebo rose; then next the hardy mate
  Crept from the sea; and in a winding cave
That scoop'd the toppling cliff, they weary sate,
And sullenly bewailed their sorrow-darken'd state.

And there throughout the lingering night, they held
  Their fearful vigils in that dismal cell;
Whilst ceaselessly without, the breakers swell'd,
  And in sonorous murmurs seemed to knell
  A funeral chant above the dead, who fell
Untimely coffined in the bleak abyss;
  Anon attentive Fancy in each swell
Caught whispers sad—the requiems of bliss—
Foretelling coming ills dark as the shade of Dis.

But Morn's effulgent light their gloom dispels,
  And wins them from their desolate abode;
Away they haste—explore the bosky dells,
  And tread the glebes with artocarpus strowed,
  Or wind the slopes where brawling streamlets flowed.
All pleasure yield; prolific Nature here
  Unequall'd gifts dispensed, and radiant showed
Her loveliest phases through the changeless year;
Adoring bent our men, and soothed their grief austere.

Fatigued at length, within a cool retreat
  They shelter seek from the meridian blaze;
A mango-wood repels the flaming heat,
  And to each breath in rustling tremor plays,
  Whilst beauteous prospects open to their gaze.
Here vernal glades in serried vistas lie;
  There palm-trees nod; here tamarinds fleck the maze;
There monkeys mewl; here gaudy parrots cry;
There solemn woods appal; here meadows charm the eye.

While thus our heroes lay upon the ground,
  Musing on what their wand'ring sight could find,
They marked a chain of hills the vision bound,
  And rise against the western sky, defined
  With striking clearness. Thence their gaze assigned,
When lo! reared on an isolated cone
  A warlike ruin stands, and to each mind
Recalls those strongholds which by age o'erthrown,
Still on Europa's lands like broken gems are strown.

And much they pondered on that ruin eld,
  And marveled by whose hands its walls were made;
Yet as they looked, Ben Nebo dazed, beheld
  The mate's stern features wear a darker shade,
  And nervous throes his stalwart form invade.
But these soon pass'd; the ruling wish prevailed;
  Both men no longer on the green-sward laid,
But rose; and by no vagueful terrors quailed,
They gained the hillock's brow and thence the fortress scaled.

They knocked: unanswered were their sounding blows
  Save by the echoes from the neighboring hights,
Or shriller cries of parrots, that uprose
  From a thick copse. Again our hardy wights
  Their summons beat; no sound; but wilder flights
Of the twice-startled birds. They knock no more;
  Ben Nebo's eye upon a pass alights;
An olive's stem from its foundation tore,
Serves at a stroke to burst the age-decaying door.

It fell: they stood within a spacious hall,
  With arms of every structure girt around;
Quaint armor rusted on the crumbling wall,
  Or clasped in moss decayed upon the ground;
  All they beheld in ruin lay imbound.
Here the last relics of a daring crew
  In this lone cell a sepulcher had found,
Whilst those who erst their hardy usage knew,
Beneath the gelid wave might ocean's floor bestrew.

Now twilight on the varied landscape fell,
  And glimmer'd through the oriel of the tower,
Rousing the owlet from his mortised cell,
  And the dim bat from sleep's occlusive power,
  On prey intent to course the nightly hour.
And then Ben Nebo marked a darker change
  Come o'er the mate: his brows despondent lower,
And aspen-like he shook; convulsion strange
In one who lustily bestrode th' uneven range.

Ben Nebo gazed upon the man askance,
  And pondered on the grief his face betrayed;
Then gently asked its cause—a frenzied glance
  Shot from the mate's dark eye; he seem'd afraid,
  But curbed his fear and then to speak essayed:
"Last eve," quoth he, "as wandering by the shore
  I pensive walked, there rose a hideous shade
From out the deep; and like a mist before
My awe-struck vision pass'd; then lost 'twas seen no more.

"Aghast I stood. But oft in years agone
 Had I unblanched beheld this goblin rise;
But now its grisled terrors smite upon
 My spirit with a frenzy, that defies
 Mere human strength. E'en now his awful size
Before me looms. Avaunt! But this despite,
 Let me rehearse a tale that sleepless lies
In memory's urn. With gory ills bedight,
Long hath it groaned within Seclusion's shadowy night.

"This tower was once a famous pirate-haunt;
 From here Blas Matsi issued for the main,
With his prize-loving lads, his flag to vaunt,
 To chase, to pillage, and by arms obtain
 From booty-laden ships the shining gain.
For years the tyrant of the flood confest,
 No hostile cruisers could his course restrain,
Fearless he roved where'er he cared to quest—
A gallant chief was he—pride of each corsair breast.

"Those were brave days: among his lusty crew
 I then a youth was a fore-top-man found;
And divers brisk affairs passed boldly through
 Had made my name above the rest renown'd,
 Whilst added wealth my rising prospects crown'd.
But yet no dreams of mere preferment rose
 With sordid pang my early bloom to wound;
I fought from instinct—loved hardhanded blows—
And felt upon the wave the equal of all foes.

"But Fate is stern: once off Gilolo's shore,
 In a smooth sea and with a sinking wind,
A British cruiser down upon us bore,
 And her broadside upon our quarter lined.
 Our men to their appointed posts assigned
Stood to their arms, all resolute, prepared
 To rake the Briton, till her lads should find
That rogues could do what rogues had ever dared,
And when their blood was up for man nor devil cared.

"The battle opened; and a cannon shot
  Dread-whistling bold Blas Matsi overthrew;
And prone he gasped upon the fatal spot
  Where he had often taught the foe to rue
  They e'er assailed him and his daring crew;
But ah! his loss we vainly could repair;
  In nautic skill—in gunnery—but few
His equals were; in danger first to dare;
He well could guide the bark and guard the secret lair.

"He fell; two rivals for his post arose:
  Dave Vangs, a son of rude Northumbria's shore,
Whose cutlass foremost gleam'd in battle's close,
  Unwilling sheathed till hope of blood was o'er;
  Next to the chief a second rank he bore;
Yet as command the general voice conferr'd,
  So none by right of station ever wore
The chieftain's plume. To Vangs the most demurr'd—
A flinty hearted man who mercy deemed absurd.

"His rival was myself. I simply placed
  My cause in deeds and not in vainful boasts;
I, too, as oft the jaws of danger faced,
  And burthened Stygia with untimely ghosts,
  When foemen trespass'd on our guarded coasts.
Our claims acknowledg'd, lots by all were drawn,
  And soon the issue reach'd th' assembled hosts;
Vangs, who ambition lured, had learned to fawn,
And gained by specious arts the men he held in scorn.

"He won; but still the action was opposed,
  And discontent prevailed among the crew,
While those who hated him, together closed,
  And swore that ere the waning moon was new
  He should his transitory honor rue.
I counselled peace, and sought by every wile
  To quench the murmurs that portentous grew;
But all in vain, for as we made the isle
We rose in arms and wrought in true seafaring style.

"I can recall the deed, though years in flight
    Have borne it to the cloudy past away;
Still now it rises in rekindled light
    As plain as if it happed but yesterday.
    For there are things that never can decay,
Though deep we hide them in negation's mine;
    And when we deem they are unspeaking clay,
They wake and fright us with a voice malign,
And in their sinewy coils the stoutest heart entwine.

"As sunk the Pleiads in the leaden brine,
    And winds blew light from Oyolava's land,
The signal rang; and bent on ill design
    In grim array appeared th' rebellious band.
    To strife they fell; dealt with such lusty hand
That at their mercy soon the vessel laid;
    But still unconquered Vangs applied his brand,
And on their ranks a dread impression made;
The bravest at his rage uncertain stood dismay'd.

"At once the jarring rovers to compose,
    And bring the Briton to an early peace,
I headlong pushed among the clenching foes,
    And shouting, bade the work of carnage cease.
    The combat lulled; and as by slow degrees
Order returned, I challeng'd Vangs to try
    A single combat. Flash'd like fire his krees,
And dark his scowl and fierce his angry eye;
Ere long we closed in wrath—to conquer or to die.

"With cruel force my foeman plied his brand,
    His blood was hot in ire; the fiery glow
Of his wild eyes gleam'd wilder, as his hand
    That oft had caused the gory streams to flow
    Aimed to inflict a last—a fatal blow.
In vain I sought to beat his strokes aside,
    My arm was powerless 'gainst so dread a foe,
And when at length a desperate lunge I tried,
I caught his point and fell, bathed in a crimson tide.

"My wound was sharp. All feeling fled before
  The shock that paralyzed the vital stream;
And senseless to my berth the seamen bore
  My blood-grim'd form. There with uncertain gleam
Life's taper burned. At length the doubtful dream
Passed o'er, and by degrees my strength renew'd.
  But fast in durance pent, no sunny beam
With genial warmth—Nature's inspiring food—
My energies awoke, by mingled ills subdued.

"Thus I remain'd, whilst on our course we stood—
  Bound homeward to our long-forsaken isle—
When one dark night, as in a dreary mood
  I sought in sleep my anguish to beguile,
  I heard o'er-head, shouts, maledictions vile,
And Vangs' deep voice o'er all arising higher;
  Intent I heard; and in a little while
The awful truth flashed on my senses dire;
Grim fear upon me seized—the vessel was on fire!

"In frantic rage my prison bars I beat,
  For now the boats were filling with the crew;
Each moment too, increased the scorching heat,
  As more abaft the flames devouring flew;
  And then I gazed my cabin window through,
And felt augmented horror o'er me creep,
  As swift the boats receded from my view
Across the smooth and molten-bosomed deep;
Anon for help implored or hopeless sank to weep.

"But sudden on my ear there fell a sound
  Of oars, and gazing o'er the lurid tide,
Amid the pitchy smoke that drifted round,
  A boat with one lone oarsman I descried;
  Hope flashed anew. My voice for aid I plied;
He heard—he paused—then swiftly row'd away.
  I thought him gone; but soon the door awide
Was thrown, and ere I could delight betray,
Dave Vangs himself appeared my terror to allay.

"Forth through the suffocating heat he led
Me to the pinnace, and when set within,
With nervous strokes across the deep we sped;
For ever and anon—with sounding din—
Shot from the heated guns began to spin
Above our heads. Beyond this cannonade
We paused to watch the fiery demon win
Its rapid way. Ere long the flames invade
The powder store; and lo! in ruin all is laid!

"We suffered much; but as the wind was fair,
Held the light skiff before the veering foam.
Three days elapse; when, through the ambient air,
Like a blue vapor, loom'd our islet-home;
And just as Twilight's glimmer 'gan to gloam,
Shot o'er the bar and moored upon the strand,
Thankful for life—resolved no more to roam
From the safe-circuit of the genial land;
Thus musing hied away and pleased each object scann'd.

"With weary feet we sought this lonely tower,
Where fixed remained a section of our band
To guard the spoil, lest in an evil hour
Invasive keels should pass the circling sand,
And fell possession of the isle demand.
To these lorn comrades we rehearsed our tale—
So sad but few its influence could withstand—
And mingled with the dull vibrating gale
Was manhood's broken groan and woman's plaintive wail.

"But who with heart a-breaking, most bewailed
The missing brave, who most in pity sighed,
Like thee, Timandra! Thou whose glance assailed
My inmost soul, that conscious vainly tried
To turn the woe-presaging shaft aside.
Thou fair Timandra, how I worshipped thee!
How for thee suffered, since my hand was dyed
With that red stain which blots whate'er I see,
And conjures goblins foul that rack me hideously!

"Ah, well I loved thee! For thee I yearned
    With an intensity, hot as the rays
Of Barca's sun! Ay, loved when passion spurned,
    Merged into one fierce bolt—one hellish blaze
    That still within my scorching bosom plays!
But why arouse the dead? Why from their tomb
    The spectres of a grisled past upraise?
What though Vangs won thee? In nocturnal gloom
Deep in yon stagnant pool he met a murderous doom!

"I slew him; and his gurgling sobs, as crept
    The whelming eddies o'er his gelid mold,
Into my ears like stygian peans leapt.
    Fierce was my joy; and short as fierce, there roll'd
    Amid those strains a subtler note that told
Of peace departed. From that hour I bore
    The mark of Cain, that where, or sea or wold
I chanced a fugitive to wander o'er,
Confest my crime—that crime that steept my soul in gore.

"It matters not to tell how I escaped
    From this curst isle—the region of that crime:
Or how through weary years my course I shaped.
    Until besprinkled with the frosts of time,
    A hopeless man, I sought this lonely clime.
'Twas tenantless. Amazed I groped around,
    And near yon palms that to the sea-winds chime,
I, choked with grief, espied a grassy mound
Marked by a wooden cross with clustering blossoms crowned.

"'Timandra's grave! Amid the clasping turf
    She sleeps in trance unbroken—sleeps though shrill
The keen winds whistle—and the rumbling surf
    Sonorous thunders; or from yonder hill
    The cowering birds with cries the concave fill.
She sleeps! With her my fondest hopes are laid,
    With her shall they remain, entombed, until
Th' imperious voice of Fate shall bid my shade
Launch from its ashy coil and ghostly realms invade!"

The pirate ceased: as closed his story grim,
　　Aurora smiled above the eastern hills;
The woods resound, and through the azure dim
　　In golden eddies foam the moaning rills.
　　Nature awakes; her pulse the landscape thrills,
And all with life inspires. Our men uprose
　　And hasty sought their cheer. Ben Nebo wills
The forest to explore—thenceward he goes;
His comrade into life the arid tinder blows.

Anon when rural fare their hunger fed,
　　The circumjacent lands around they rove,
And jocund view spontaneous bounties spread
　　O'er mountain, glen, and solemn-looking grove.
　　Long thus they rambled, till a thicket wove
With heat-excluding woof, to rest invites.
　　Here stretch'd at length, across a glassy cove,
They saw astounded, from the neighb'ring heights,
Titanic moas wing their long, laborious flights.

While thus in idlesse prone the seamen lay,
　　Watchful of what their vision pass'd before,
Ben Nebo's thoughts were wand'ring far away,
　　And often sought his long forsaken shore—
　　That shore which he might never visit more.
And musing thus his thoughts began to lower,
　　Congenial to the winds, that whisp'ring o'er
The distant seas, sighed thro' the nemorous bower,
And filled with pensive dreams the spirit-soothing hour.

Then Nora's charms in added freshness rose,
　　And woke to voice the love-inspiring song;
From his distilling lips the measure flows
　　In nervous verse—in mellow tide along,
　　As thousand beauteous scenes his fancy throng.
Of love he sang, whence sprang its mystic birth,
　　Its mystic chain that binds the weak and strong,
Or bends to anguish or exalts to mirth,
All that as mortals press the air-suspended earth.

As the sweet image rose before his mind-—
  Thought he, no other with such charms could vie;
For Love is selfish, arrogant and blind,
  And prone to cheat the most experienced eye;
  Besides, by nature being rather sly
He rollicks in a good, clean-cutting jest,
  Nor cares how deep love-smitten creatures sigh;
How swains go mad; how feverish maidens rest;
Or how the grandam coos with spasms in her breast.

Ere yet the crescent reached the middle dome,
  Both heroes trod the steep-ascending road,
Rejoiced to gain their rude, but friendly home,
  And cast aside their heart-oppressive load
  In slumber's torpid spell. But dreams forebode
The wished enchantment; troubled they repose;
  Within each sleeper thoughts tumultuous rode—
In slumber-breaking hosts—presaging woes
Portentous which no mere word-painting can disclose.

Ben Nebo vainly sought to fall asleep;
  Keen were his senses—feverish they wrought
In tempest visions such as darkling sweep
  Through some Byronic soul by Angels taught
  To sing the terrors of Immortal thought.
He tost, he murmur'd, as along they cours'd,
  Till all the darkness seem'd with spectres fraught;
Then, horrified, from his deep silence forc'd,
He hailed his comrade: long the two sad men discours'd.

And thus the mate: "Perchance these dreams are sent
  As subtle warnings of some peril laid
By foes unknown, yet primed with fell intent
  Our lives to end. But by this mystic aid
  We may the dangers of the hour evade,"
He said. The twain uprose; throughout that night
  With nervous steps bestrode the dewy glade;
When in alarm Ben Nebo saw a light
Fixed on the barren shore below the turret's hight.

He then his comrade hailed; both men alarmed
   Gazed on the light, which, as the air was clear,
Proved a huge fire, by wild-men lit, who swarmed
   Around the whirling blaze in rude career.
   Till dawn our sailors watched in livid fear
The blacks carouse; when in periguas stowed
   They stood away. Once from the island sheer,
Our seamen to the smould'ring embers strode,
And there beheld a sight that man's foul nature showed.

There, cast about the ashes, did appear
   Fragments of human flesh; dark clots of gore
And bones black-singed, grim relics of the cheer
   Which had sufficed the cannibals, when o'er
   The waters roaming, on this lonesome shore
They landed to partake their hideous fare.
   Sick at the sight our heroes homeward bore,
Musing on what they saw; and loth to spare
The next swart troop that should invade their lonely lair.

But scarce they left the foul-ensanguin'd scene,
   When Nebo roused a black, who fast asleep
Had laid a copse of sago-trees between.
   Woke by th' intrusion, with a sudden leap
   He rose, and fled so swiftly, as to keep
Our seamen far behind, though hot to slay
   The flying wretch. At length a rocky steep
Enveiled him from pursuit. There hid he lay
Till the blue waters drank the fading hues of day;

Then cat-like out he came. In quest of prey
   He sought the offals of the ghastful feast;
But by our heroes seen, they dogged his way
   As hunters dog some dread, ferocious beast,
   Nor till the spot was reached this duty ceased.
But as from out the wood they boldly prest
   The savage turned—his inky visage creased—
And ere a death shot could the deed arrest,
Th' illfated mate received a javelin in his breast.

As sinks the shotted corse beneath the wave,
  So sank the mate at that death-dealing blow;
Yet ere his spirit to the winds he gave,
  Ben Nebo's musket laid the slayer low—
  Yet poorly recompensed his poignant woe.
Then on the mate's remains he sadly gazed,
  And mused on things but the afflicted know—
Things that grim-shapen nigh his reason crazed,
Which doleful Horror from his devilish gulfs upraised.

All things must perish. Once their work is done,
  All in negation must dissolve away;
The noble oak when its last sand has run
  Shall only later than frail man decay;
  But later still the Pyramids shall lay
In atoms prone, and Earth, still later rent,
  Shall like these all Destruction's law obey.
All, all must perish, such their chief intent,
From chaos first they came in chaos to be blent.

Ay, all must perish: nought of earth can stand
  The ever-gnawing tooth of deathful Time
That eats into all things. Man's temples grand;
  His proudest columns; empires reared sublime;
  The mind's great efforts; Nature's wonders prime,
In his sharp fang succumb. Thus Allah wills—
  They rise spontaneous; at th' appointed chime
Expiring sink. The mightiest globe that fills
The depthless void for naught its wondrous power distills.

'Tis evening's hour. The dying orb of day
  Veils his last gleam beyond the purple sea,
As sad Ben Nebo wends his lonely way
  Down the steep hill and o'er the winding lea,
  To where a trench beneath a rifted tree
Wide-gaping yawns. Here must the mate repose;
  His oft-selected tomb, and near where she,
Timandra, whom he loved, when living chose
As her eternal crypt when life's black dream should close.

Whilst his dull task the pensive man pursues,
  Excursive sorrows through his bosom stream;
Again the chequered past his mind reviews,
  And scans a length'ned waste, where scarce a gleam
  Of light breaks thro' the gloom—where horrors teem,
And all is turmoil, doubt and wretchedness;
  Such the dark thoughts—unlit by cheering beam—
That his afflicted spirit earthward press;
Until he doubted life and longed for nothingness.

In vain! Who can reverse his orbit here,
  Or guide his being as his sovereign mind?
Who shape his course as his own timoneer,
  Or sail without an over-ruling wind—
  Who mauger Fate can journey unconfined?
Man's but the toy of an omniscient power,
  Whose foresight hath his farthest acts designed,
Hath sent him here to mewl his little hour,
And wither at a blast like the frost-bitten flower.

His day is closed before his Morn's begun—
  Ere yet the grain is ripe the scythe resounds—
At one fell swoop his life-inspiring sun
  From beaming light into grim darkness bounds,
  Like downy-blossomed plants o'er meadow grounds
By winds impelled, his flying years succeed,
  One raven shadow all his sky surrounds,
And dim the ray that may his spirit lead;
Here till his work be done, unhappy man must bleed.

Yet Allah ruleth all—in Him we move,
  In Him our being have, our bents pursue;
He prompts to toil, he leads mankind above;
  He bathes the landscape in its varied hue,
  And wheels the stars etherial orbits through.
All, all are full of Him: the Seasons raise
  Their thankful homage as they sweep anew;
And man, vain man should join the votive praise—
Extolling the great Source, of all that he surveys.

The crow is chanting on the rifted ledge,
    Loud-roarings echo from the deep, where white,
'Gainst billow-breaking rocks along the edge.
    Hoarse beats the surge. No more in serried flight
    The wild-ducks fly; but on the sheltered hight
Condensed await in expectation still
    The gathering storm. Anon in rising might
Upsurging ocean chafes; shores whistle shrill;
Crags moan; woods nodding roar, and howls the topmost hill.

As night o'er all her sable mantle spread,
    Ben Nebo sought the solitary tower,
And whilst the embers weird reflections shed,
    He close-encoiled in Retrospection's power
    In doleful thought beguiled the wintry hour;
No soothing slumber lulled that thought to rest,
    But fiery pangs his deepest soul devour;
Love still a vigil kept within his breast,
And by the sounds without still deeper was imprest.

Imbound in moody dreams he drooping bent
    Before the lurid and inconstant blaze—
Heedless of all—on his own woes intent—
    Though rude without the blust'ring tempest plays,
    And blows the flame a thousand different ways.
But he, sad hermit in his ruined cell,
    Disowns the present, and the past surveys;
By sorrow taught within himself to dwell—
He breathed on earth but lived in climes invisible.

www.ingramcontent.com/pod-product-compliance
Lightning Source LLC
Chambersburg PA
CBHW020030030726
47499CB00007B/2356